Fighting the Japanese in Burma

BLOW THE BRIDGE

A true story leading up to the demolition of the Sittang Bridge and its aftermath

Lance Corporal CG Nicholls
2nd Battalion Duke of Wellingtons

Pen Press Publishers Ltd

First published in Great Britain by
Pen Press Publishers Ltd
39-41, North Road
Islington
London N7 9DP

ISBN 1-905203-33-0

Printed and bound in the UK

A catalogue record of this book is available from
the British Library

Cover design by Jacqueline Abromeit

To the hundreds of my mates who lost their lives in Burma I dedicate this short story, may they rest in peace.

Fighting in the jungle was no "picnic"

About the author

CG Nicholls was called up for service in the Army in 1940. Although he was concerned that the war would end before he could get into uniform, in fact, he served six years, four years in India and Burma, finishing up in Germany and France.

Two years ago, after much persuasion from his wife, he decided to write this book in tribute to the 400 out of 600 soldiers of the Duke of Wellingtons Regiment who were either killed or taken prisoner.

Foreword

Today, it is difficult to imagine just what it must have been like in the war years of 1939 – 1945 for young men sent to the battlefields.

This story tells of the conflict in the Far East and one particular young man thrown into a theatre of War totally alien to his lifestyle in England.

Can we imagine, being a 20 year old who had never stepped foot out of the country never mind seen a jungle, then suddenly transported half way around the world, to fight the might of the Japanese army?

These pages contain the personal account of a young man's journey of adventure against the background of one of the bloodiest campaigns of the Second World War.

It is a story of bravery and survival with human touches of warmth and laughter; it is also a story of inequality of armies and at times total chaos.

I hope for anyone who reads this story it will be enjoyable, uplifting and a thoroughly good read.

The "Dukes" cap badge that we wore with pride

Table of Contents

Preface

At 11.15 am on September 3rd 1939, the Prime Minister of the day, Neville Chamberlain, broadcast to the nation in a voice charged with emotion: *"I am speaking to you from the Cabinet Room at 10 Downing Street. This morning the British Ambassador in Berlin handed the German Government an Official Note stating that unless we heard from them by eleven o'clock that they were prepared at once to withdraw their troops from Poland, a state of war would exist between us. I have to tell you now that no such undertaking has been received and that consequently this country is at war with Germany"*.

We were stunned as we listened to our wireless sets and contemplated how a war with Germany would affect us personally.

As a young man of 19 it was pretty certain that I would be involved in one way or another.

My father had been a soldier in the First World War in the Artillery, so maybe I would join the Army and follow in his footsteps.

Chamberlain did not have the steel to lead the country and a new leader had to be found quickly.

There was only one man with the qualities needed for this job and Winston Churchill was summoned by the British people to lead them through some of the darkest hours this country had ever known.

Three days after taking office, when he made his famous "blood, toil, tears and sweat" speech to the House of Commons, he went on to say, "You ask, what is our policy? It is to wage war by sea, land and air, with all our might and with all the strength that God can give us; to wage war against a monstrous tyranny. Victory, however long and hard at all costs will be achieved."

'Cometh the hour, cometh the man', seemed to sum up the new Prime Minister, Winston Churchill, who was not a young man and had fought for his country in the 1914-18 war.

In 1940 there was still a threat of invasion from across the Channel against a Britain whose Army had lost most of its equipment at Dunkirk and whose new divisions were largely untrained.

France had capitulated and it was vitally important that her Navy should not be allowed to fall into enemy hands. As a result the Royal Navy were compelled to fire on French warships at Dakar and Oran. The French losses were catastrophic.

The bulk of our Fleet was concentrated at Scapa Flow in the Orkney Islands to strike if the German Navy put to sea.

Meanwhile our Merchant Shipping was suffering terrible losses, particularly in the north Atlantic through U-Boat warfare.

Brave sailors risked their lives to bring the essentials we required to fight a war.

Winston Churchill asked President Roosevelt of the United States of America for the loan of forty or fifty of his older destroyers until our new ones began to come off the slipways of the yards where they had been laid down at the beginning of the war.

The air battle was assuming ever-greater proportions as the Germans launched wave after wave of their vast Airforce against us.

At night when the sirens sounded, families would make their way to their gardens to take cover in Anderson Shelters which were cold and damp but offered protection from bomb blast.

I volunteered to train as an Air Gunner in a bomber but owing to a mix up in my Army Medical I was turned down. I wonder what would have happened if a career in the Royal Air Force had been my fate?

Our gallant young airmen were making sortie after sortie every day but there was a limit to their efforts in human exhaustion and aircraft.

From unsuccessfully trying to knock the Royal Air Force out of the skies and thus open the way to an invasion the Germans switched their tactics and launched the blitzkrieg against London and other targets giving our fighter and ground staff just sufficient breathing space to build up strength and resources again.

Looking back on that period it is almost unbelievable that any one man could have stood up to such a strain as the nations war leader, yet Churchill never flinched.

In one of his famous speeches, which everyone always listened to intently, he stated that, "We should fight on the beaches, we should fight on the landing grounds, we should fight in the streets and in the fields".

After Britain and France had declared war upon Germany following the invasion of Poland in September 1939, there was little real activity on land which would suggest that a state of war existed. Belgium, Holland and Luxembourg were neutral, and although the Allies expected a replay of the World War I plan of a "right hook" attack by the German Army through Belgium to trap the Allied forces east of Paris in a vast encirclement, the Allies could not respond, until the Germans moved, without violating the neutrality they were avowed to uphold.

The "Hook Plan" was essential because the virtually impregnable Maginot Line was erected on the German-French border.

It was an elaborate system of deeply buried fortifications erected after World War 1.

The British Expeditionary Force under its very able commander, Lord Gort, and the French Army prepared to face the mighty German war machine.

Because of the speed and force of the German advance a plan was put into action for the BEF to fall back on the coast at Dunkirk and be evacuated by sea.

In disarray, individual units retreated to the coast, none of them knowing where their fellow troops were or how great would be their chance of escape.

Allied troops poured onto the beaches through the burning rubble of Dunkirk, exhausted from days of frantic defensive fighting only to have to stand and wait under a hail of shells and bombs from the dive-bombing Stukas wailing overhead.

Supplies and rations were running out and the demoralised and hungry men could only hope for rescue to arrive in time. The thought of facing imprisonment or massacre if they lost the race against time caused a sense of panic.

Meanwhile, the Royal Navy at home had been far from idle. Since 20th May 1940, Admiral Bertram Ramsay, the Flag Officer, Dover, had been gathering together a motley fleet of coastal ferries, six coasters, 16 barges and 40 Dutch Lighters. Only one flotilla of Destroyers was available to protect the evacuation craft.

Experienced naval commanders from the first rescue ships brought news that Dunkirk town was a shambles.

As soon as the veil of secrecy was lifted and the news of Operation Dynamo broke on 31st May many boat owners simply set sail. This huge civilian effort lifted 26 000 men from the beaches in addition to the 72 000 already evacuated.

When Dunkirk's remaining defenders surrendered early on the morning of 4th June, 338 226 men had been saved. In all, 289 tanks, 63 897 vehicles and 2472 guns were left behind. The Royal Air Force flew a total of 4822 operational hours during which they destroyed 258 enemy aircraft and damaged 119 more for the loss of 87 of their own.

Under threat of imminent invasion, a new British spirit came to the fore, inspired by Churchill's firm leadership.

Everyone found rationing a nuisance, however in Britain the same rations were allocated to all, with the exception of children, who were entitled to extra foods such as milk and orange juice.

On an average week you were able to purchase for each person one egg, two ounces of butter, two ounces of tea, half a pound of meat with a sausage thrown in if you were lucky, two ounces of cheese and whatever you could scrounge or buy to give your family a substantial meal.

Meanwhile in the Far East the majority of Japanese were agreed on the necessity for expansion from their overcrowded islands but were not sure in which direction Japan's destiny lay.

In the 1920s the expansion was limited to peaceful commercial penetration of the Chinese mainland but this soon accelerated and was pursued by force of arms.

The army believed that Japan's interests would be best served on the mainland of Asia, but it was open to question whether Soviet Russia as well as China should be the target.

The navy felt that all their needs could be satisfied by a policy of southern expansion into the mineral and oil-rich areas of South East Asia and the islands of the southwest Pacific.

In August 1936 a compromise was reached between the army and the navy to expand eastwards and southwards at the same time, a course that would ultimately lead to war with the Western powers.

By 1937 a full-blown war against China was put into operation and despite Japan's supremacy this war dragged on until 1945 mainly because of the resources of manpower that China possessed.

The Japanese were keeping a careful watch on events in Europe where Germany's success in the defeat of France and the Netherlands and the preoccupation of Great Britain with the Battle of Britain and events in the Middle East provided the opportunity that the Imperial Navy had been waiting for.

Surely with their massive naval power there would be some easy pickings and they licked their lips with great anticipation for their future expansion.

Of course I never for one moment dreamed that I would be involved in the war in the Far East and that there would only be a very slim chance that I would return unscathed.

If the Japanese had not decided to go to war I could have had a very interesting and comfortable time outside of Europe and would never have known the true meaning of battle for survival.

In July 1940 the elated military reconstructed the government putting Prince Konoye in as Prime Minister and Matsuoka as Foreign Minister.

These men were little more than tools of the military and they turned a blind eye to the build-up of Japanese forces.

At the same time, negotiations took place in Berlin and Moscow for alliances that would give them a free hand to escalate their military expansion in South East Asia and the southwest Pacific.

Joining Up

In 1940 when I was twenty I waited with great expectation for the postman to bring me a brown envelope from the War Office which would inform me where I would report to start my war-time duty. My main worry was that the war would be over before I could get into uniform.

Five years of my apprenticeship to become a Compositor had been served when I received my Call to Arms and duly arrived at Plymouth Barracks in August 1940.

With the Germans preparing for an invasion on the other side of the Channel I would be right in the firing line if it happened and apart from a few under strength Divisions backed up by Dad's Army we should have great problems holding back the mighty force of Panzers.

Every night we would stand too on the beaches wondering what would happen if the Landing Craft suddenly appeared out of the sea.

Had the Germans appeared with their Panzers, blasting away our chances of survival would have been practically nil but they didn't and we survived.

Training in the fields around the Barracks, our eyes wandered into the clear blue sky where the British and German fighter planes circled overhead trying to shoot each other down.

We were kitted out in khaki uniforms and all the odds and ends that make up our kit were dished out by the Army stores.

We were not allowed out of barracks very often but I did manage a trip to the cinema to see The Invisible Man, with Claude Rains, it was different and I quite enjoyed it.

Once a week pay parade took place and I marched smartly up to the officer in charge of paying out and received fourteen shillings for my trouble; this was about 70p in today's money. Later on I was getting a pound a week, which was quite adequate for my social life.

After a few months in Plymouth the powers that be decided to send us north where we could be trained to fight and shoot when the enemy decided to invade.

Yorkshire was our destination and the mill town of Halifax where the Duke of Wellingtons Barracks were situated, was to be our new home.

Roads out of the town centre were mainly uphill and we marched up them many times during our training but our leg muscles were getting strong and it proved no problem.

It was very cold in the winter of 1940 and Yorkshire was far enough north to feel the brunt of the weather.

One winter morning, we left the barracks by coach and drove across the Moors to an area where a rifle range had been set up. The ground was a blanket of snow and lying on it trying to hold the rifle steady took all our concentration, but we were quite satisfied when it was over and a hot drink was very acceptable.

There were plenty of dances either in the barracks or in the town and the Mill Girls enjoyed dancing with the soldiers.

I remember Christmas Day, 1940, not so much for the dinner and usual trimmings but for what happened in the evening.

Our Platoon was not allowed out of barracks over

Christmas as we were on fire duty and we were not looking forward to spending the evening chatting among ourselves.

There was a six-foot steel fence all round the barracks and one of the lads who had been wandering around outside came in and said that a couple of young girls were asking if some of the lads would like to go to their house nearby where they were having a party. Two or three of us who fancied the challenge of climbing the steel fence said we would like to join them. Of course if we were caught out of barracks when we were on duty it would have meant a Court Martial, but what the hell!

We thought the risk was worth taking and helped each other over the fence and joined the waiting girls.

They were a typical Yorkshire family where the men folk were serving their country somewhere or other but the mother was pleased to see us and we enjoyed her home cooking.

A few drinks and some simple party games and we thanked them for making us feel welcome and departed ready to climb back over the fence and went to bed quite happy with our Christmas Day.

About ten of us were put on a signals course where we learned Morse code, which took a little time to grasp.

The secret of Morse code is not to count the dots and dashes but to recognise the letters and figures by the sound they made through the earphones and after a couple of months I was able to take and send messages at a good rate and fairly accurately.

With my initial Infantry training over my overseas adventures were about to begin.

We Head For India – August 1941

To bring the 2nd Battalion Duke of Wellingtons, stationed in India, up to war-time strength, 100 volunteers from the "Dukes" headquarters in Halifax, Yorkshire, set sail from Glasgow, down the Clyde, in a 16 000 ton liner which was packed with various units of many nationalities.

Sailing down this narrow river, the navigation of this massive liner had to be precise and the pilot on the ball.

We were soldiers, not sailors and in a rough Atlantic Ocean were soon struck down with seasickness as the ships wallowed and zigzagged continuously to avoid U-Boats.

It is said that a small percentage of sailors are always seasick at the start of a voyage, if this is so I suggest they change their jobs for that is something I could never get used to.

The toilets were soon blocked with bodies and I climbed the iron steps and went to the ship's guardrail and put my head over the side.

The sickness lasted for about three days during which time we wanted to die. The relief when we were finally back to normal and being able to eat again was wonderful.

Of course, for those that were immune to the rocking and rolling of the ship, they were able to tuck in to as much food as they wanted while laughing at their mates who were a ghastly shade of grey!

While the officers took over the cabins, we men slung hammocks in the bowels of the ship where portholes were permanently sealed.

Getting in and out of a hammock can be quite tricky, but when you were settled in they were very comfortable and the slight movement of the ship soon sent you to sleep.

Unlike the Americans, in the British army the distinction between officers and men was vast and they were treated with great respect by us soldiers.

We had our meals on a trestle table and sat on wooden forms with the basic knife, fork and spoon, but no condiments. Someone on each table went to the ship's galley and picked up a tray of food and staggered back with it to the cheers of the men, we were hungry and ate anything. In complete contrast, for their evening dinner the officers could select from a peacetime menu with a bottle of wine. They were dressed in their best uniforms which their batmen had ensured were spotless and seated in the ship's naval officers dining hall.

We wondered sometimes if they were in a different army to us, but this segregation bred obedience to orders and at their command we would not think twice about what danger we might be in because this is what made the British Army the best in the world with the Germans and Japanese coming a close second.

We soon got our sea legs and started to enjoy life on an ocean liner. Three weeks after leaving Scotland we dropped anchor in Freetown Harbour on the west side of Africa.

From the ship the harbour looked very colourful with all sorts of trees and shrubs and the natives going about their daily work.

Apart from the first few days it had been a fairly smooth trip and over the ship's Tannoy there was a message saying, "are there any Compositors on board". I volunteered my services and spent some days in the ship's printing room setting menus for the officers and a news sheet for the men, it was interesting and work that came easy to me.

Bartering with the natives, who surrounded the ship in their homemade canoes, caused much merriment and helped pass the time.

We dropped a basket over the side attached to a long rope and they would fill the basket with fruit and shout out what we owed them, we usually paid them otherwise there would be a torrent of abusive African language.

Leaving Freetown we sailed south watched over by the Royal Navy. Under a tropical sun we saw Dolphins jumping out of a tranquil sea and any thoughts we may have had about war were becoming a distant memory.

Crossing the equator we were entertained to the Neptune ceremony, which was fun for the watchers but an ordeal for those taking a ducking.

The jewel of South Africa, Durban, was reached after six weeks sailing from Glasgow but not before we had rounded the Cape of Good Hope where massive waves towered over the ship, but by then we were immune to seasickness.

We were genuinely greeted by the South African people who invited us into their homes, showering us with great generosity and kindness. Many of the thousands of troops who were fortunate enough to spend some time in Durban and Cape Town, were so impressed by the country that they went back after the war and settled there, bringing up their families in this idyllic setting.

A ride in a rickshaw pulled by a Zulu in national costume was a great experience, especially when travelling along wide streets with impressive buildings and beautiful flower gardens on either side.

Every morning we were there, the people of this port would line up at the side of the ship and invite us to their homes, which was lovely for us.

Reluctantly we said goodbye to Durban and made our way across the Indian Ocean to the "Gateway of India", Bombay, after helping ourselves to crates of oranges that were too ripe to export.

An overcrowded teeming city of millions, yielded up obnoxious odours, fly's pitched on our sweaty faces and had to be knocked off. The sacred animal of India, the Cow, walked undisturbed along the pavements and we had to stand to one side to allow the smelly beasts to pass and then avoid the mess they left behind.

A train with little creature comforts, steamed out of Bombay, it was ensuite, a hole in the floor. Great dexterity was required to perform over this hole while all the time the train shook and groaned from old age.

We were staggered as we travelled along to see the hovels the majority of Indians lived in, they were probably used to the conditions, but in comparison our homes would have been like mansions to them.

Every bit of floor space on the stations that we passed was taken over by Indians who lived where they slept and obtained their income from carrying passengers' luggage, usually on their heads.

On wooden seats we travelled through scorched, barren, flat countryside, finally arriving at New Delhi, the capital city.

Not to be compared with New Delhi, Old Delhi is a walled city with great historical interest and looking the same as it had done for many hundreds of years. Both cities lie alongside each other and a greater contrast could not be found.

But we were interested in New Delhi which was to be our temporary home. It was colourful, clean, with wide avenues of tree-lined streets, and the magnificent Viceroy's Palace where the "Dukes" were on continuous guard duties.

Sergeant Jefferies, who had been responsible for our training and welfare during the voyage, made sure we marched smartly into the peacetime barracks, the 100 reinforcements had arrived and we were proud of our appearance.

Can you tell which is the "Char Wallah"

We were split up and allocated to the four Companies, A, B, C and D. We were soon training with our newfound colleagues and taking part in sports such as hockey and football. A swimming pool, which was available at anytime, was very much enjoyed in the heat.

If someone in authority had decided that all soldiers should be able to swim many lives would have been saved in the future.

A welcome cup of "char" with my mate

Two-floor spacious barrack rooms with highly polished floors that you could eat your dinner off, comfortable beds with clean white sheets, Punkas, like huge carpets swished continuously overhead keeping us cool, this was utopia and would suit us for the duration of the war.

We gradually became acclimatised to the heat of an Indian summer. The sound of "Char Sahib" greeted us in the early morning as the ever-present "Char Wallah" hovered over us with "Eck Anna" or a large mug of tea for "Doe Anna", it might be stewed but it was hot and wet and available any time of the day.

If you agreed to it an Indian barber would shave you with a cutthroat razor just before you woke up in the morning, sounds bizarre to have an open razor poised over your throat but we accepted it as part of daily life.

To get down to reality, we had to face the fact that Japan was putting into operation its plans to dominate all of the Far East and they were doing a pretty good job of it.

News filtered through to the senior officers in December 1941, that Malaya and Singapore had fallen to the enemy, after that it became a catalogue of disasters for the Allies.

As it could affect the war situation in the part of the world we were in I think the reader would like to be reminded of the terrible naval tragedy that unfolded in early December 1941.

The Prince of Wales, Repulse and four Destroyers left Singapore as Force Z, heading up the northeast coast of Malaya.

A couple of days later at 6.30 a.m. a signal was received by Force Z to say: "The enemy is making a landing 140 miles north of Singapore, investigate and deal with as the situation requires."

Prince of Wales catapulted off one of her planes on

reconnaissance. Z Force were an inspiring sight, a Battleship, Battle Cruiser and four Destroyers hoping to smash into Japanese landing parties and their escorting warships. Nothing was sighted and they returned to third-degree readiness. Suddenly the Jap air force appeared overhead flying in perfect formation, low and close. They broke up only when forced to do so by shellfire.

The Prince of Wales was first to be attacked and Repulse second, the destroyer screen they left alone.

Prince of Wales opened a shattering barrage. A bomb hit Repulse on the deck and it went through the port hangar.

By now 40 Japanese torpedo-bombers had been in the attack. Prince of Wales was hit by a torpedo and she listed to port.

A new wave of planes appeared and the end was near for the "Prince" as she turned slowly over on her port side, her stern going under. The crew were able to walk down the side of the ship to the sea.

Captain Tennant of Repulse was saved but Admiral Sir Tom Phillips on the Prince of Wales, who obeyed the out-dated tradition which says the senior officer must go down with his ship was drowned as were a great many sailors whose naval careers were brought to an horrific ending.

This single engagement gave Japan supremacy over the Pacific and Indian Oceans, for the British it was a catastrophe of major proportions, both strategically and psychologically.

On the financial side we lost millions of pounds in just a few hours and these glorious warships were not replaceable for many years.

This disaster was unknown to us at this time and we were happy with our lot.

Apart from guard duties at the Viceroy's Palace we were having a great time in New Delhi, swimming in the pool, hockey games in which I seemed to end up as goalkeeper most times and which I found rather dangerous with the hard ball flashing past my head too often.

A trip into the town for a Chinese meal, to which I was rather partial, was a treat for us soldiers who had been used to good food in the UK but which lacked variety.

We had a good running track, which was used considerably and in which I was very interested as I found out that I was a good runner and invariably won the races in which I competed. This was to prove of great help when I was in the jungle and probably saved my life on many occasions.

We had a canteen run by Indians which supplied beer at a reasonable price and which we retired to most nights invariably ending with a punch-up but it was good fun.

All in all life in New Delhi was excellent and if it had not been for the Japanese we may have sat out the war and thought that war was not that bad after all.

But the war clouds were gathering in the Far East and although we didn't know it at the time we were really living in "Cuckoo Land".

Gradually, we noticed a change in attitude to our training. For instance a plan was devised by the senior officers to improve our fitness, this involved marching for some hours in the blazing hot sun in full kit, then to improve our military skills we were issued with spades and picks and told to dig trenches, while the officers stood around with supercilious grins on their faces, wondering what part of their Sandhurst training covered this excellent plan. The icing on the cake was when the senior officer present at the site, at the end of the day, gave the well thought out order: "fill in trenches, prepare to march back to barracks". The looks on our faces showed what we thought of this comedy of errors but we dare not say anything.

We repeated this for three consecutive days when we had a break before going through the same routine; those that survived this ordeal were as tough as old boots and ready to take on any challenge thrown at them.

At last we had to say goodbye to New Delhi with the hope that one day in the future we would come back as civilians for a holiday in this lovely city.

The powers that be, decided to move us to Peshawar on the North-West Frontier of India; this seemed to be an excellent move, there was nothing but desolate open space and would be great training for our future jungle fighting!

The barracks in Peshawar were not in the same class as those in New Delhi, but they were built to house a battalion with all the services that were required to make a soldier's life tolerable.

The tough Pathans, who inhabited this rugged part of India, were not averse to breaking into the barracks and stealing any of our equipment they could lay their hands on.

Every night our rifles were locked in a rack in the centre of the barrack room and the lights were kept on, but even with this tight security some rifles mysteriously disappeared and were soon in the hands of a tribesman.

There was a bazaar in the centre of Peshawar, nicknamed by us as "Loose Wallah's Bazaar", where if you were unfortunate enough to have had a piece of equipment stolen you could purchase a similar piece for a token sum from a grinning Pathan.

Winter on the Frontier was inevitably moving on and it was suddenly Christmas Day 1941, and a Company of the 2nd Battalion Duke of Wellingtons Regiment, of which I was a Private Soldier, were seated in their dining hall expectantly looking forward to their festive dinner, which in Army tradition was to be served up by the NCOs of the Company.

We were surprised when in marched our esteemed Battalion Commanding Officer, Colonel Basil Owen, followed by his senior officers, this was not Santa Claus with his sack of goodies, this was serious and we were desperate to know the reason for his visit.

The Battalion Sergeant Major, resplendent in his finest uniform and peak cap with cane tucked tightly under his arm quickly took control of the proceedings and in his finest barrack square voice he shouted out: "stand to attention for your Commanding Officer". With a mighty clatter every chair in the hall was pushed back and as one we stood to our full height, wondering what was going to happen next.

The Colonel and his Officers positioned themselves at the top of the hall and our much respected Colonel said: "enjoy your Christmas for I have to inform you on good authority that within three months the Battalion will be in action against the Japanese forces in Burma".

When the Colonel left we sat down to enjoy our festive dinner, with all the trimmings, not letting this dramatic news spoil our appetite.

Many of our troops were married with young families and although the thought of getting some action thousands of miles away from the European theatre of war was extremely exciting we had to face the fact that we could be wounded or killed in action and wives and children would be left without their bread winner.

We had experienced nightly bombing raids in the UK by the Germans and seen the exhausted troops coming back from Dunkirk but fighting the Japanese in the Burmese jungles completely bewildered us.

Who were these little fanatical "Japs" who were smashing all the resistance that we could put up against them?

Could they be stopped in the steaming hot, malaria infested

jungle by a proud Yorkshire regiment who were now on intensive training on the barren North West Frontier. We realised we would only be a small cog in a large machine, but many cogs could build up into a strong force.

Around about this time I was struck down by my first dose of malaria but was well looked after in the military hospital where liquid Quinine was poured down my throat at regular intervals, not an acquired taste.

A few days after leaving hospital I rejoined the Battalion who were training in the wild, rough, mountainous North West Frontier.

One morning as we assembled before starting out on an Exercise we were fired on by Pathans hidden up in the hills, we only had one casualty which strangely enough was a lad near me who had a finger shot off, we opened up with a barrage of rifle fire that soon had the tribesmen running for their lives.

I was amused at the toilet facilities here, although I know you are not really interested, it was an important aspect in our lives in India. Anyway whether you are interested or not I am going to attempt to describe it.

A circle was drawn in the open about twenty yards in diameter, poles were put about three yards apart and a roll of canvas, four feet high, was placed around the poles. Inside the canvas about twenty toilets were installed facing inwards and some rolls of paper placed in the middle. Eventually I had to go to the toilet where I was shocked to see that nearly all the seats were occupied, what a sight! Trousers down, bare bums showing, strained faces. I slipped quietly on to a vacant seat and feeling embarrassed quickly eased down and when finished slipped out in great haste. I thought this might make you smile, as there is not a lot of light amusing incidents in this story.

From the tented camp up on the frontier that had been our base for a few weeks we marched twenty miles back to barracks where we arrived exhausted and with blistered feet, but happy to resume normal training in Peshawar.

Only a week previous I had left hospital after my bout of Malaria so I considered I had done well to march twenty miles on rough tracks under a scorching sun and in full kit. I was certainly very fit and this was to be a great advantage in the months to come.

This is the massive country that we were expected to defend against the might of Japanese forces

Burma Here We Come

When Winston Churchill looked at a map of the Far East he could see that the Japanese were moving forward at a frightening rate and that the Port of Rangoon, in Burma, was our last means of getting in reinforcements while we still had use of it. We desperately needed Infantry, guns, tanks and ammunition if we were to stand any chance of saving Burma.

Back in Peshawar the Duke of Wellingtons Battalion were ready to march to the railway station where a special train had been put at their disposal to take them to the port of Madras in Southern India.

We marched out of the Barracks led by our Colonel and it was a very impressive display for the watching crowds, 600 soldiers heading for action in Burma, not knowing at that time that only 200 would survive the ordeal.

Although this was an emergency it took the train ten days to cover the journey.

The steam train chugged along at a steady speed and we passed the time, sat on wooden seats, by playing cards and chatting among ourselves.

When the train stopped in between stations we would take it in turn to get some boiling water from the engine to brew a mug of tea.

We had the usual Indian luxuries with a hole in the floor for a toilet and washing was very difficult with limited water.

It was very hot and we were grateful for the shade the carriage provided and the breeze coming through the windows, which had no glass in them.

It was not possible for us all to sleep on the seats so some of us stretched out on the floor and woke up covered in bruises.

From Peshawar the train travelled through Rawalpindi, Delhi, Allahabad and many other places right through the length of India.

There was some light relief when we stopped at many stations where all sorts of food and drink were brought to the carriage. A mug of tea, eggs on toast, fruit that had to be peeled for hygiene and anything the vendors could persuade us to buy.

The port of Madras in the far south, which was our first destination, was extremely hot and we lined up at the docks ready to board the ship that would take us with our equipment across the Bay of Bengal to the Port of Rangoon in the Gulf of Martaban. The ship had to sail 1000 miles to reach this destination.

Once more we slung hammocks in the bowels of the ship. We were getting used to it and this time we were not plagued with seasickness, probably because our travels through the Atlantic Ocean and the Indian Ocean had made us better sailors, not forgetting that the seas were much calmer.

To pass the time we played Bingo on deck, this was fun and took our minds off what the future warfare had in store for us. I didn't win anything but that did not worry me, as I had nothing to spend it on anyway.

America was very concerned that Rangoon was kept open as long as possible so that essential goods and weapons could be transported along the Burma Road into China where they would be used to continue the fight against Japan.

The Burma Road was an incredible feat of civil engineering that ranked alongside the Great Wall of China, for it had been built by thousands of coolies without the aid of any mechanical equipment. Mile by mile they had hewn through solid rock in the hills and mountains with primitive picks, shovels and rock-crushing hammers, carrying away the earth in baskets, to prop up the red soil and prevent landslides.

It had been completed at the cost of countless lives in September 1938, and in the spring of 1941 the United States Congress had made its first Lend-Lease allocation of nearly 5 000 000 000 dollars in aid to China.

Prior to our arrival the enemy had already started to infiltrate into Burma with their main objectives being Rangoon and the oilfields in the north of the country. What an achievement it would be for the Japanese if they could capture these two important landmarks intact.

If you look at a map of Burma you will see that it is shaped like a hand with a long index finger pointing southwards. As the human hand divides into fingers so does Burma, split into ranges stretching southwards with the mighty rivers, Chindwin, Irrawaddy, Salween and Sittang running between them. This comprises the bulk with the forefinger stretching down the western shore of the Malay Peninsular towards Singapore.

Burma is where India and China meet and was once described, because of the malarious and inaccessible hill tracts, as "one vast military obstacle". It is as large as England and France combined. Victoria Point, the southernmost tip, is within six hundred air miles of Singapore. The northern limits, twelve hundred miles away, include great peaks reaching 20 000 feet glistening with eternal snow.

The country was hot and steamy but with breath-taking

beauty, a land of golden-domed pagodas and saffron-robed priests, with an abundance of game and wild life, plus fishing and shooting. On the material side it boasted vast oilfields, silver, tin, copper and tungsten, vast forests of teak, precious stones, wolfram, rice and rubber.

When you think of the great assets of this country it is not surprising that the enemy would do anything to capture it.

For the infantryman it was both jungle warfare and European type warfare; at one moment in the open, with good observation but exposed; at another, in thick jungle, concealed, but with limited visibility.

The importance of Burma to the Allies lay in its geographical position. As long as Burma was held, India was safe. Calcutta and the great industrial centres of northeast India were practically immune from air attack, and eastern land frontiers were secure from the threat of invasion. Also through Burma lay the only route by which the Chinese armies could be kept supplied and the American air bases in China maintained. It was essential that China should be enabled to continue her struggle against Japan and thus contain large enemy forces.

The Governor of Burma was Sir Reginald Dorman-Smith who lived with his family in Government House, in Rangoon. A monstrosity of a building, with large, lofty rooms and long echoing corridors, where an army of uniformed servants, who moved as silently as if on well-oiled castors, waited upon their every need.

Then in the same building were the Divisional Commissioners, District Officers, Forestry Officers, Senior Police and Railway Officers.

In December 1941 the Army in Burma was unfit for war with a major military power and the country was unprepared to face invasion. To make matters worse, there was no effective intelligence organisation in Burma. As a result, little or nothing was known of the Japanese forces, their positions, movements, strengths or intentions.

Before concentrating on the Indian Army and their ability to hold back the enemy a mention could be made about the part China would play in the coming battles.

If the Allies lost Burma the American supplies travelling along the Burma Road from Rangoon into China would cease immediately, so Chiang Kai-Shek, the Chinese supremo, decided he wanted to get involved as soon as possible.

General Wavell, our Commander, was aware of this situation and discussed the offer of Chinese troops with the Governor, Sir Dorman-Smith, who was obliged to point out that from the civil point of view the offer was not as good as it looked. Letting Chinese forces into the country might be unpleasant. How would they treat the Burmese population? They were said to be ill equipped, ill-trained and ill-disciplined in comparison with troops under British command.

But no immediate plan for protecting Burma without Chinese aid seemed feasible, so General Wavell flew to Chungking to consult Chiang Kia-Shek. The Chinese were our allies and they had been fighting Japan for years.

A definite offer of the Fifth and Sixth Chinese Armies was made to Wavell and he at once accepted the aid of the Sixth Army who was already on the Burmese frontier.

The only troops available to defend Burma at this time were the 17th Indian Division commanded by Major General Jackie Smyth.

A character reference of this General is necessary in order to understand the calibre of the man who was given the job of holding back the hordes of fanatical Japanese now pouring into southern Burma.

He was aged 50 and was a regular soldier who had service

in both World Wars and seven Indian Frontier campaigns.

The supreme award of the Victoria Cross and the Military Cross, with six mentions in dispatches, showed terrific bravery.

After commanding a Brigade at Dunkirk with distinction, he was given the task of leading a very inexperienced Division in Burma.

In later years after leaving the Army he became a journalist and broadcaster, Military Correspondent to the Sunday Times and several other newspapers and then an author.

He wrote 32 books including children's books, cat books, lawn tennis books and particularly military history and biographies.

In politics he won Norwood for the Conservatives and remained their M.P. for 16 years.

He was blown up by shells and mines in the early trench warfare days of 1914-15 in France.

The worst disabilities he suffered resulted from an anal operation in Quetta, India, in October 1941, and the illness, which followed the Burma campaign of 1942.

He fought back from these problems and eventually led a full life as a civilian.

Fate was not kind to him for he suffered a terrible tragedy when his eldest son, Captain John Smyth, was killed in action at Kohima, in Northern Burma, when the campaign was turning in favour of the Allies.

General Smyth's 17th Division was a very young unit only partially equipped and completely untrained as a Division. Its battalions had no experience of Jungle Warfare; fighting in the jungle needs special technique and pack transport.

This unit had been trained as a mechanised Division, which means you tie it irrevocably to a road because; only by means of that road can you supply it.

These were the only troops available and 17th Division was sent into action against an enemy who thrived in living on the land and moving easily through the jungle.

General Wavell who was in overall command regarded the Japanese as a second-class enemy; in fact, the Japanese Imperial Army with its savage and completely fanatical infantry element, constituted as formidable an enemy as had ever been faced by any Indian or British forces. They believed it was the greatest honour they could achieve to "die for their Emperor", but we did what we were ordered to do and prayed that we would survive the war and that one day be reunited with our loved ones.

17th Division, commanded by Major General Jackie Smyth, were in position from the Sittang Bridge down the east side of the river to Moulmein which was being threatened by the advanced troops of the enemy.

Three Brigades were the total force of the Division; they were 48 Brigade under Brigadier Noel Hugh Jones, 46 Brigade under Brigadier Roger Ekin and 16 Brigade under Brigadier John Jones.

The 1/7th Gurkhas, of 16 Brigade, who had been pushed up front to hold the Japs at Moulmein, fought with great tenacity. When they ran out of ammunition they fought with rifle butts, kukris, boots and fists. Gurkhas always went into battle led by British officers and this was a great combination as Officers and Gurkhas were prepared to die for each other.

General Wavell and General Hutton, who were the senior officers, in desperation impressed on General Jackie Smyth the need to fight as far forward as possible and even counter-attack whenever he could.

This was against a far superior force of two Divisions of battle-hardened troops ready to die for their Emperor.

How General Smyth would like to have signalled back:

"give me the tools and I'll do the job", but his discipline as a regular soldier ensured that he would obey orders and carry on regardless.

The Japs had reached Moulmein where the forward troops of 17 Division were fighting "tooth and nail" to slow them down and hold on as long as possible but with no immediate reinforcements it was merely a delaying tactic and the Division moved back to Martaban.

If General Smyth had been in overall control he would have swiftly moved his troops back to Bilin-Kyaiko-Sittang area as a preliminary to a defensive wall centred on the Sittang Bridge but he was completely overruled.

The War Office were coming out of their nightmare and sending out desperate signals all over the place for reinforcements of any shape or size to get into Rangoon before it was lost to the enemy and there was optimism among the Generals that if this happened we could hold back the two Japanese Divisions that were sweeping all before them.

While 17th Division were struggling to hold Martaban, into Rangoon harbour slipped three Infantry Battalions, the 2nd Duke of Wellingtons (my regiment), 1st Cameroonians and the 1st West Yorkshire Regiment.

The 1st Royal Inniskillings, an Irish regiment who were in India, were put on standby to be flown into Northern Burma at a later date.

In a race against time, before the Japenese overran the Port of Rangoon, the Saviour of the Burma Army arrived. It was the 7th Armoured Brigade who had been fighting the Germans in the Desert when they were whisked out of the front line and moved with great haste to the quickly assembled ships.

The 7th Armoured Brigade comprised some very fine names which would give any General great confidence in his forces, they were the 7ᵗʰ Queens Own Hussars, 2ⁿᵈ Royal Tank Regiment, 414 Battery Royal Artillery and the 95ᵗʰ Anti-Tank Regiment.

Without this fine Brigade of tough and experienced troops there is no doubt that we would have been defeated and destroyed in a very short time.

The Brigade docked in an eerie silence, broken only by the clanking of the ship's donkey engines and once by the wail of an air-raid siren. The scene was one of gigantic desolation. Huge warehouses stood with their doors open and vast quantities of stores of all kinds, lease-lend weapons for China, lorries, food, ammunition, beer and champagne, lay intermingled, half in and half out, some of the cases broken open and their contents scattered over the ground. There were no guards, no labourers, nobody to organise the unloading. For the first time in its history the great port of Rangoon was idle, derelict and deserted.

Among the few figures waiting on the quay was Brigadier Anstice, the inspirational leader of 7ᵗʰ Armoured Brigade, who came on board at once and explained the military situation.

There was a lot to be done before the regiments could be ready for action. But worst of all was the total absence of dock labour, both skilled and unskilled, and it was no small achievement by the soldiers and the merchant seamen that in little more than forty-eight hours the ships were cleared.

At 4 pm on the 23ʳᵈ the commanding officer was hastily summoned to brigade headquarters. The situation on the Sittang was critical, Rangoon was in danger, the brigade was to move at once.

Meanwhile the Japanese High Command, surveying the situation in Burma, were jubilant as they swept aside the token resistance of a mixture of British, Indian and Gurkha troops who were not trained or equipped to stop this onslaught in the jungle.

The Japanese 33rd and 55th Divisions both took the offensive, without waiting for the arrival of their rear echelons, to drive the British from the line of the Salween and Sittang to swing north to Toungoo, destroying any Chinese forces opposing it, and for 33rd Division to make a rapid advance towards Rangoon where the British and Indian forces were to be overcome. 33rd Division was to establish a base at Rangoon for later operations in central and northern Burma.

Although the strong reinforcements had arrived they were not yet available and General Smyth wanted to withdraw his 17th Division across the one bridge over the River Sittang and fight the Japs on the open country on the west side of the river but again his reasoning was not acceptable to Generals Wavell or Hutton.

Smyth's 17th Division, having withdrawn from Moulmein and Martaban, was struggling along the cart track heading for the Sittang Bridge without knowing that the Japanese 33rd Division was forcing itself through the jungle to the east of the track in order to get to the bridge and cut off the escape route.

Anyone who was not able to reach the bridge would have to attempt to cross a deep, fast flowing and treacherous river nearly a mile wide in places.

To add to all these other problems our troops were bombed and strafed by a Jap Air Force that had complete control of the skies.

Not an officer or man of the "Dukes" had ever seen a Japanese soldier or a jungle, but they were all ready and eager to fight.

"Dukes" D-Day

Here is a tale of unbelievable disaster. The accounts of endurance, desperate bravery, and comradeship, serve only to underline the bitterness of the defeat. There was no shame for The Duke of Wellingtons, in fact there is much that will be remembered with pride, yet it is not a campaign that can ever be regarded with glory.

After disembarking from our ship we were moved into barracks outside Rangoon where we checked our rifles, Bren guns, mortars and all our kit. This was to be the last time for six months that I would sleep in a bed of any kind in future until we reached Assam (which is now Bangladesh) it was a case of folding a blanket and laying it on the ground. I was usually so tired that I went into a deep sleep.

The first evening some of the more adventurous "old soldiers" decided, come what may; they were going to have an enjoyable night on the town. When we asked them what would happen if they were caught out of barracks and arrested, their retort was: "so what, it would be better than getting killed in action". I didn't think it was worth the risk and I would accept what fate had in store.

After a few days we boarded a train, which took us over the River Sittang Bridge, on a narrow gauge railway, deep into jungle country to face the enemy.

We didn't realise as we crossed the bridge, which was a massive structure of metal girders that we would not come back over it again, but that was not in our thoughts at this moment in time.

One Company was placed in position near the bridge to support the Indian troops already there.

On paper the reinforced Burma Army was beginning to look formidable enough to presage the end of the disasters, in fact the disasters were only just beginning.

It was pitch black as we steamed through the jungle and our hearts beat a little faster as we wondered what fate had in store for us when the train reached its destination. I gripped my rifle and pulled my helmet on tight as I sat on a wooden seat in a compartment surrounded by troops of my Company completely bewildered at the circumstances we now found ourselves in.

The way our Battalion was mishandled still beggar's belief 60 years after the event.

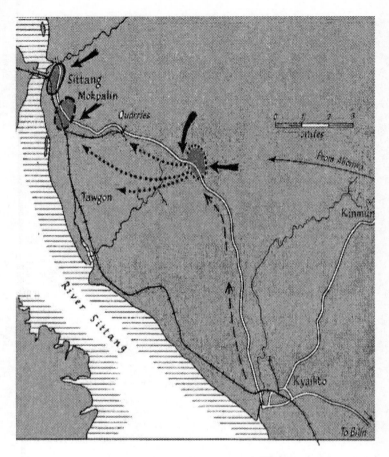

SITTANG BRIDGE

Sent up from Rangoon the previous day, the most obvious task for them would have been to dig themselves in round the Sittang bridgehead. Instead they were bundled on to Kyaikto, detrained on 20th February and ordered to withdraw to the Sittang 18 hours later. Within that time they had lost most of their weapons, all their transport, all their kit and upward of 300 well-trained and well-officered troops. God alone knows what the "Old Duke" would have said about it had he still been alive.

On arrival in Kyaikto as far as outward appearances were concerned we looked infinitely more battle worthy than the other men of 17th division, we were well nourished and freshly shaved, our khaki shirts and shorts had been put on not later than the day before, our hose-tops and puttees were neat and our boots, although dusty, serviceable and recently studded, every man had a new steel helmet and we frequently burst into raucous song for no attributable reason.

The main part of our Battalion was composed of regular soldiers, most of whom had not seen a lot of action during their long service, some had signed up for twenty years and were looking forward to being discharged with a pension in the near future. To make up the Battalion to full strength there was us war-time only soldiers who tended to look up to the "old soldiers" who we considered to be professionals, not part-time as we were, but when it came to fighting we proved to be their equal.

The distance from Kyaikto to the Sittang Bridge is about twenty miles. The Sittang is a big river, which is crossed at a narrows a few miles above the estuary by a railway bridge, which had been adapted for road vehicles by the sappers.

By no stretch of imagination could this track, which we were about to take from Kyaikto to the Sittang Bridge, be called a road, for the surface was loose dry earth dotted with occasional tree stumps.

The undulating country in these parts was covered with dense scrub jungle, although near Kyaikto there were some rubber plantations. These consist of tall straight trees planted in geometrical rows and devoid of undergrowth.

Anyway to get back to the story; we quickly moved to a clearing in the jungle, I was ordered to get in position behind my Bren gun, which I always had great confidence in, and with my mate to assist me I quickly whipped on a magazine and peered into the black night with the realisation that there was nothing between us and the enemy. So this was real war, something we had only read about in books or seen in films, would the Japs suddenly appear in front of us? Would they shoot or bayonet us? We would have to shoot first and stop them in their tracks or we were dead.

Entrenching tools were in short supply but we knew that the shallowest hole in the ground trebled our chance of living in this inferno of shot and shell and we dug feverishly with bayonets and bare hands.

We kept awake and alert through a long dark night, finger on trigger, safety catch off, but apart from some firing away to our left we passed a peaceful night although occasionally to break the monotony we would have liked to have had an excuse to blast off some ammunition, but these thoughts soon passed.

War is a strange thing and fate had destined that one of us laying behind this Bren gun all night would be killed in a matter of a few weeks, which of us it would be was something we never even thought of, why should we.

Back home no one would know that my battalion was in danger of being attacked, as we spread out to stem the enemy and stop them advancing any farther.

The German war at this time was in limbo with both sides building up their forces and we were the ones in danger of losing our lives in the Far East.

Daylight was a welcome relief and we were ordered onto the road, which was no more than a cart track. We moved off in Companies, single file, with one section on one side and the next the other side, through a dust corridor hacked through the jungle from Kyaikto to Makpalin walled by high trees and scrub jungle.

It was difficult enough for marching soldiers but extremely hazardous for vehicles.

The heat was intense under a cloudless sky and the dust thrown up by our boots and the wheels of the transport grinding along at two miles an hour completely obscured the track ahead and clogged our ears and throats and made breathing difficult, the sun sucked moisture from our bodies already short of water, every step required an effort of will power, leaving little in reserve to concentrate on the ever-present danger of ambush.

As we moved back along the track in the early morning Japanese fighter aircraft put in a long and vicious machine-gun attack, although the casualties in our Battalion were quite light several of us had miraculous escapes.

Formations of bombers came over at very frequent intervals to drop their bombs after which the escorting fighters dived down to machine gun us. It was only after hours of this drastic attack that we realised that we were the targets for both air forces.

One of our lads who was not as young as some of us was obviously exhausted and gradually dropped back, this could be fatal so we took it in turns to get either side of him and helped to keep him going. This camaraderie was very prevalent among the lads and it was great to know that you always had a shoulder to lean on.

Approximately every hour we would get the order, "halt, fall out", when we would sit on the side of the track and get our cigarettes out. The danger of getting lung cancer from smoking never occurred to us, we were only interested in surviving the next few hours. Nowadays those who smoke are told to kick the "filthy habit" but in those days no one was concerned and we smokers were thought of as heroes to fight for our country.

After marching all day, exhausted, we rested in a rubber plantation where we queued for a mug of tea which was the best we had ever tasted, so we got back in the queue and had another.

We tried to keep our spirits up by chatting to each other and laughing when someone came out with a funny remark but our thoughts were on what would happen now, the officers were in the dark about future plans so we had no chance of getting any information.

It has been claimed that twenty-four hours were lost in organising the withdrawal. Wavell's Dispatch says it was "badly mismanaged by HQ 17 Division". Davies, Hutton's BGS, described it as "disgracefully mismanaged". The grounds for such severe criticism are not easy to establish. Smyth had wanted to get away behind the river Sittang days before either Wavell or Hutton would agree to do so. As it was, Hutton's written permission did not arrive until the evening of 19th February, after which orders had to be issued and brigade commanders briefed. By then it was dark, several units were in close contact with the enemy, communications were appalling and everyone was tired, hungry and thirsty. The first stage of the withdrawal, was fifteen miles away, with wounded to be carried and transport to be negotiated over chaungs and the bunds between paddy fields. Many of the troops had been engaged in battle for as long as seventy-two hours.

BURMA 1942
The Japanese Invasion Routes

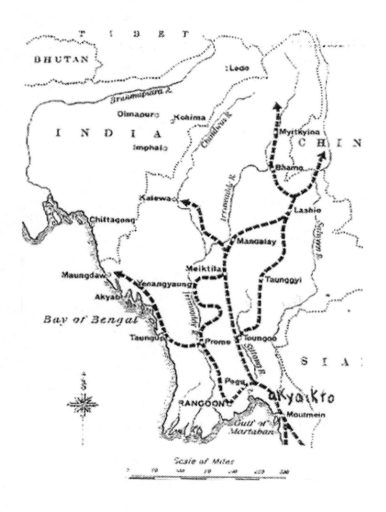

After Kyaikto, it became incomparably more difficult. The single track, unsurfaced, pockmarked with bomb craters, barely wide enough for one vehicle to pass another, with those ambulances carrying wounded given priority. We were hedged in by jungle so thick that men easily became lost if they wandered far from the track. Control over any sub-unit much larger than a platoon was virtually impossible.

The Japanese air force, hovering over the retreating columns was not having things all there own way. A private of 2nd KOYLI (Kings Own Yorkshire Light Infantry) with a machine gun shot down a fighter plane to the accompaniment of tumultuous cheers. One of my mates in the Dukes also shot down a plane that had been shooting at us. It turned out to be an RAF machine, but we were not to know that and the effect on morale was electric.

During the evening in the rubber plantation as we relaxed there was a roar of approaching engines, which caused a sudden rush to a long trench that went right through the area. Most of us reached the trench before fighter planes swooped over, very low, with machine guns blazing, the crash of bullets nearly bursting our ear drums and although it only lasted a short time it was a frightening experience and we breathed a sigh of relief when it was all over.

When the planes passed over we looked up at them in disbelief, someone shouted out: "the bastards are our own planes," surely enough there was the RAF markings on their wings.

Some of our lads were killed or wounded in the attack and these were the only planes we saw in the whole campaign that carried the RAF markings; in future it would be the big red circle that would take control of the skies.

To be fair to the pilots, the map references they were given were completely wrong and they were exonerated at a court of inquiry.

I was so tired that I just collapsed on the ground and was soon in a deep sleep not wanting to know what lay ahead.

Had we known that nearly 200 of our Battalion of 600 would die within a couple of days we should not have slept so soundly and we would have stayed awake worrying about how our families would take the tragic news that they would receive.

Next morning we moved out of the rubber plantation back on to the dusty cart track several miles from the bridge and safety.

We were now part of 46 Brigade who were rearguard and being pressurised by the Japanese 33rd Division close behind. Meanwhile General Wavell and General Hutton struggled to find a solution to a catastrophe of their own making.

General Wavell

Once more in the increasing heat we trudged along towards the bridge. General Smyth was still optimistic that his 17th Division might yet win the race to safety, but he observed that it was going to be "a near run thing".

I was very fit and the physical part of the job was no problem but I was naturally apprehensive whether my days were numbered, but with my mates around me we kept our spirits up and even managed a burst of singing from time to time.

We had no ideal as regards the strategy that the Generals had planned for us and our little world was confined to a part of the track we were on and the jungle on either side, so we just gripped our rifles with bayonets flashing in the sun and plodded on.

Throughout the night and the morning the Sappers toiled at making the Sittang Bridge, consisting of eleven spans, each of 150 feet, ready for demolition. Explosive charges were placed on the upper and lower booms and by the late afternoon of the 22nd February all that was left to reduce the Sittang Bridge to a tangled mass of steel girders was the formality of lighting the safety fuses.

The Brigadiers of 48 Brigade, in the lead, and 46 Brigade at the rear, did not realise that a gap of a mile had developed between the Brigades. The Japanese 33rd Division, which had moved swiftly through the jungle to the east of us, were quick to exploit the situation by pushing in troops to set up a road block, covered by mortars and machine guns.

When I was called up for the Army, and sent to India, I didn't think for one minute that I should be involved in any real warfare. In the blink of an eye my life was about to be changed.

The Japs were waiting for us and as we rounded a bend they had the leading troops, which were us, in their sights and let fly with everything they had.

Their intention was very clear, they were going to kill as many of us as they possibly could, that was their job, but we had to escape from this bloody chaos if at all possible.

The noise was horrific as bullets smashed into us, and mortars exploded too close for comfort. We dived into the jungle and opened fire with rifles and machine guns, we were not giving in without a desperate fight and hopefully our bullets found their mark on these fanatical little yellow men.

The Japanese invasion of Burma happened at a frightening pace

The battle of the Sittang was "a dog fight in the jungle", and no one who took part in it would quarrel with this assessment, for men fought with animal savagery and died in their hundreds with little idea of what was happening around them. Although it virtually decided the fate of Burma it was short in duration, but time in the strict sense had ceased to exist for the soldiers involved. Night or day made no difference, the fighting was non-stop and in its closing stages it developed into an intense battle for survival with everyone's hopes pinned on one thing, getting over the bridge to link up with the 7th Armoured Brigade in order to fight a battle on more equal terms. The weary troops, who were ambushed, shelled, mortared and bombed almost every yard of the way, had fought themselves to a standstill, yet they responded to the rallying calls of their officers with great courage. In many cases they were out of touch with Brigade Headquarters, but they were still confident they could make the bridge, now just a short distance away.

The battle can be reckoned a defeat, if not a disaster, but it was redeemed and raised to the height of victory by the magnificent courage displayed by the officers and men including the Duke of Wellingtons. This was our first battle, fought under conditions completely foreign to the Northwest frontier training, which we had undergone.

Hardly any of us young men had heard a shot fired in anger but we fought to the end against highly trained veterans of crack Japanese divisions.

A First Aid Post was set up by our medics to combat the terrible punishment we were receiving, there were men with lower jaws blown away, cavernous stomach wounds and limbs, so shattered, that only immediate amputation could save their lives.

This is the brutal side of war of which there is no glory but something that every soldier was faced with.

A Captain who had been responsible for us during our voyage to India moved up alongside me and I shall never forget the grim determination on his face as he fired his revolver with the style of a cowboy in an old western film. I hope he lived to remember this moment.

The jungle was so thick that we could only see a few yards in front of us, so we just fired indiscriminately to our immediate front and I was as scared of the bullets coming from behind as I was from those coming from the front, I didn't want a bullet in my backside, how would I explain that away?

Japanese officer surveys Sittang Bridge

Sadly, from the occasional screams, I knew enemy bullets were hitting some of my mates. Mortar bombs were exploding perilously close and as I moved forward a blast from one of these bombs hurled me from one side of the narrow track to the other. Dazed and confused I feared the worst, but I picked myself up, got hold of my rifle and moved into the jungle once more, but this time on the west side of the track.

How did I feel at this moment in time? I was not afraid, perhaps a little confused, but ready to take the fight to the enemy. My knees and hands were bleeding but in the heat of battle I didn't feel any pain.

My family back home would not have had any ideal of the danger I was in and that at this moment in time I could be wounded or killed.

A Gurkha ready for action

The Japs were firing with rifles and machine guns and we were forcing them back with everything we had.

The difference between the Japs and us was that they were battle-hardened troops with no fear of dying but for the majority of us it was our first battle experience.

We had to move along this track if we were to get to the bridge but the Japs weren't giving an inch and would sooner die than let us pass.

A quick glance about 50 yards up the track, showed a tragic sight: Four Indian soldiers, with bayonets fixed, all dead and laying in the same prone position. They must have been machine gunned down when moving abreast, ahead on the track. It must have been a quick end; they wouldn't have known what hit them.

A chill ran down my spine as deep in the jungle to my left a Gurkha battalion in our brigade went into action with a blood curdling war cry that frightened me, and I was on their side. I couldn't see them because of thick jungle but I pictured them with Kukris flashing, fearlessly charging forward, killing any Japs in their way, led by brave British officers. Gurkhas were held in high esteem by British troops and a bond of friendship that had always existed carries on to this day.

The enemy was being forced back gradually but at a high cost to the Gurkhas who were showing the Japs that they were their equals when it came to bravery, they were fearless.

For some unknown reason I found myself alone just inside the jungle; for the first time in my life as I gripped my rifle with bayonet flashing in the sun I would have willingly killed any Jap who got in my way, but instead I came face to face with a Gurkha who had been shot in the chest and was bleeding profusely. He looked at me for some kind of help, I handed him my water bottle and he gratefully took a drink and staggered on looking for some medical help, but he was in a bad way and I would be surprised if he survived this horrendous injury, his family would be devastated when they received this terrible news.

With the track completely blocked by the Japs there was only one way to go, through the jungle towards the River Sittang.

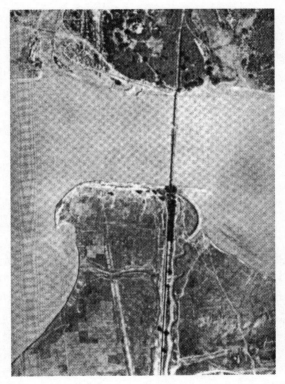

The Sittang Bridge at the narrowest part of the river

When every nerve is tensed ready for instant action, eyes ready to notice the least movement or note any sign of possible danger, ears atoned to hear every smallest sound, with an enemy likely to be met at any moment, movement through

45

the jungle is physically and mentally exhausting. Just one companion would make so much difference. There is a longing to get into a hole and hide or to turn back to where friends are known to be. He must be a brave man to walk through the jungle alone when he knows that the enemy will be on the alert.

A terrible decision had to be made by General Smyth, if he blew the bridge he sacrificed the bulk of his Division. If he failed to blow the bridge and it was secured intact by the enemy the way to Rangoon lay open.

At 05.30 hours on Monday 23rd February, Major Orgill and his Sappers blew the bridge over the River Sittang and I was on the wrong side. Every man in the force new what this meant, the great railway bridge had been destroyed and there was no hope of getting over the bridge.

After the mortaring and shooting it was absolute chaos, small parties of British, Indian and Gurkha troops were forming up in any small clearing they could find.

The group I became attached to moved off along a track that must have been used by Burmese for many years.

Without warning heavy firing from the jungle in front of us caused terrible panic and we hit the ground, life was precious to us and we were not standing up to be killed. A few minutes before I met up with two of my friends I had travelled from England with, Benny Abramson, a Scout leader and Eddie Bailey, a true Devonian. When the shooting started they took the full force of the firing and they were killed or taken prisoner, they were never heard of again, I was sorry for their families, they were great lads and I sadly missed them. Recently, I obtained information on when they died, Eddie was killed a few hours after I left him and Benny died later. (See appendix).

Before we sailed to India, Benny invited Eddie and myself to his home in Leeds, where I met his family. We didn't know then that only one of us three would come back but we were not contemplating this and had a very nice tea.

Recently by a strange coincidence a friend of mine was working on his computer and came upon the "War Graves in Rangoon" and provided me with information that I had not seen before. I thought it would be of interest to reproduce this. Benny's Christian name was Barnet and Eddy's was Edward. I can only assume that Benny was taken prisoner and probably died a year later in a prisoner of war camp. Eddy died shortly after I last saw him but whether he was shot or drowned I may never know. (See appendix).

I was stunned when I saw this because I had thought about them quite a lot and as in many instances since wondered if it was fate that I was still alive and that so many of my mates were dead, I guess it was not for me to reason why but to carry on doing the job that I had been trained to do.

Survival was the order of the day and when the Japs stopped firing we moved quickly along tracks in the jungle that we hoped would lead to the river.

Mile after mile we trudged along with British, Indian and Gurkha troops all mixed up. All along the tortuous route to the river the jungle was catching fire, and the crackle of burning bamboo was indistinguishable from rifle shots.

Sometimes we were heading down narrow tracks and when these were too narrow we hacked through jungle, the Gurkhas were usually in the lead as they could use their kukris to good effect.

We came to a small clearing and stopped to get our breath back while looking for someone we might know, a friendly face could mean a lot.

We were a small group of twenty or so mixed nationalities and I was shocked to see Colonel "Basil" Owen, the Commanding Officer of my Battalion, the 2nd Duke of

Wellingtons, who had got caught up in the chaos and now wondered what the hell was happening to his life.

Shattered from his exertions, this gentleman with great determination, said, "next time men we fight". These words will live in my memory forever, as it was probably the last command he would ever give.

He held the highest rank in our Battalion as Colonel and I was just a Private Soldier, but at this moment in time, in this situation, our eyes met and rank didn't count for much, as survival was the main objective for both of us.

Why was the Colonel of the Battalion and his Batman not accompanied by any of his Officers, of which there must have been at least twenty, or senior NCOs of which there would have probably been double that number. I would hazard a guess that this was the only time in the British Army's history where such a chaotic situation had been allowed to develop and I had witnessed this dreadful tragedy.

Some time later I learned that Colonel Owen and his Batman, made their way independently to the east bank. Assuming that the rest of the Battalion had crossed they swam the river together. On arrival at the west bank, in a state of complete exhaustion they went to the nearest village in search of food and shelter; the villagers appeared friendly and welcomed the British soldiers.

But not all Burmese on the west bank supported the Allies and there were snipers and treacherous priests, with their shaven heads and saffron robes.

Marauding gangs descended on the village during the night and murdered Colonel Owen as he slept in a hut. His batman, with most of the fingers of one hand severed by a dah slash, managed to escape. What a way for a Lt. Colonel, leader of a proud Yorkshire regiment, to finish a great career, killed by thugs. (See appendix for his memorial).

Once again I was able to obtain confirmation of the death of my Colonel, he was only 39, his wife Betty Owen and his parents must have been devastated when they received the news, I had great regard for this man.

We all know that war is a nasty business, however it is fought. There are those who seem to believe that it is better to be killed by bullets, bayonet or grenade than by atomic bomb, but death is death whichever way it arrives. Kill or be killed is a meaningless expression for those who have never been called upon to face such a stark alternative.

After marching all day along narrow tracks we reached the river as it was getting dark and I collapsed among the trees and undergrowth in company with a pal of mine, Harry Oldfield, a schoolmaster from York, who was married and had a young family, he had been on the same draft from England.

Harry and I searched in our rucksacks and came up with a tin of bully beef and some hard biscuits. When we got the tin open the liquid ran out but with what was left we made a meal which we devoured hungrily as we had not eaten since early that day. After a night under the trees where we slept soundly, we seemed to get separated and I never saw him again, he didn't make it back to the Battalion, it was pretty certain he had either drowned crossing the river or had been killed trying to get away from the enemy.

Harry was a very friendly person, well educated with a sense of humour. He never struck me as a dedicated soldier but he never shirked his duties. What a lot his teaching skills could have contributed to society had he survived the war, what a shame he died, what a waste of a university education, but that applied to many people caught up in the war.

As with Eddie Bailey and Benny Abramson the name of Harry Oldfield came up on the web and it said that he had died on February 22-23. (See appendix). It was not 22nd because I saw him on the morning of the 23rd but nevertheless he died shortly after I left him, what a strange thing war is, we never knew whether we would survive that day or the day after.

Once again it was me that survived, I was leading a charmed life, I had been with so many soldiers who had since died, so why was I still struggling on in one piece, it seemed that fate had decided it was not yet my turn and the dreaded "Reaper" had not yet looked over my shoulder.

What now? The Japs were moving in fast and were not likely to take prisoners, the Bridge was a tangled mass of steel, and the river nearly a mile wide in places was my only means of escape, what a choice.

The River of Death

As I moved to the edge of the river next morning I saw a great many men starting to take to the water, some struck out strongly with their friends, some lay on their backs hoping that the current would carry them across. Some waded in up to their waists, lost their nerve and came back again. Some headed back into the jungle hoping to find an easier crossing place farther up or down river. Some swam a few hundred yards only to be attacked by agonising cramp and drowned. Others panicked, clutched at swimming men and dragged them down. Some decided to take a chance on Japanese hospitality and sat dejected by the rivers edge.

I couldn't believe what I saw as so many tough soldiers drowned, disappearing beneath the water only a few yards from the riverbank and we seemed helpless to save them.

Instead of digging trenches and filling them in it would have made more sense to ensure that as many troops as possible were able to swim, so many lives would have been saved on this day but it seems that no one envisaged such a tragedy.

Hundreds of Indian, Burmese and Gurkha troops were hurriedly constructing rafts from everything that might conceivably float. The river was dotted with rafts and the heads of swimming men while Japanese aircraft cruised up and down machine-gunning at leisure. The average time of crossing took two hours. No boats were available; during the previous days a lot had been collected, taken to the west bank and holed in order to prevent the Japanese crossing.

The first of the wounded were arriving at the river, a pitiful collection of men, crawling, hobbling, tottering; here was Private Stafford of the KOYLI, now with only one leg, and Captain Howden with a leg so severely shattered that it subsequently had to be amputated. Here came Lieutenant Skinner of the Dukes who was badly wounded, an officer who was a real character and who I knew very well as he had been part of the reinforcements, it was hard enough for a fit man to get across the river but to rely on help from others was tragic.

In spite of their utter exhaustion, there was still plenty of fight left in these desperate men on the wrong side of the mighty Sittang. They fired at the enemy whenever the opportunity offered itself.

Officers and NCOs who seemed as confused as we were suddenly found their voices and were shouting out orders which were: "throw your equipment and rifles into the river". What sort of Army were we in that orders such as these were given to us soldiers!

We took the bolts out of our rifles and threw them into the river as far as we could together with our Bren guns, which we dismantled so that the enemy would have great difficulty using them. Boots were not conducive to swimming, so were discarded, although those that did reach the other side suffered with sore feet after walking some miles on the rough ground and would have given anything to get their boots back. If the Japs had appeared now we should literally be caught with our trousers down.

The cost of the clothes, arms and ammunition that was being dumped all around us must have been colossal and I believe that waste could have been avoided if General Smyth had been given the power to move his troops back behind the bridge days before.

As no one appeared to be taking control of us it was left to every individual soldier to decide his own fate, stay and be taken prisoner or killed, or get across the great expanse of water in front of us.

I could swim, thank God, but this near mile wide tidal river would be a formidable task, which very few of us had confidence in conquering. If I wanted to survive there was only one decision to make.

My mind was made up, I stripped down to a pair of shorts, pushing nearly all my clothes, pay book, cigarettes and all the personal things I had in my pockets, into the undergrowth and moved into the water.

A glance along the bank revealed a strange sight, soldiers in various stages of undress prepared for an ordeal not of their making and a short time later many of them had drowned.

The amount of clothing that was dumped on the river bank was enough to clothe the Burmese living in the area for years, imagine the scene as they picked over everything, trying on trousers and jackets and laughing at each other as they changed from villagers to some kind of soldiers. I don't know whether they were interested in our boots after walking bare-footed all their lives. Perhaps we started a new trend in fashion, somehow I doubt it!

This was probably the beginning of the "Charity Shops" that are so prevalent in the high streets these days, except this clothing was free, on the basis that if it fits take it.

Any help would be accepted with open arms and this appeared in the shape of a small log, which was close enough to the bank for a Corporal of the "Dukes" and I to grab hold of and push off in our attempt to reach the other side.

We held the log sideways and moved our legs up and down to get some momentum going, for twenty yards or so our adrenaline was running high, had we cleverly beaten the odds. With disbelief we felt the log sinking under the pressure of our arms, it sunk to the bottom.

We looked at each other with dismay and disappointment, after what we had been through surely we deserved better luck than this.

Now out of our depth we were faced with a difficult decision, we had only gone a few yards and the river looked massive.

The Corporal quickly summed up the situation as far as he was concerned. He said: "I don't think I can make it, I'm going back" and he turned and swam back to the bank.

If he had ordered me to go back with him, which his rank entitled him to, my story could have taken another twist, but he didn't.

I moved my arms and legs to stop sinking and watched him swimming back wondering whether I should follow him. Had he made the right decision and was I stupid to carry on?

When I was called up for the Army in 1940 I could never have visualised the desperate situation I was now faced with.

The length of the swimming bath was the height of my swimming achievement; I had only learned to swim while camping with the scouts at Churston in Devon when I was fourteen.

The Scout Master who patiently taught me to swim wouldn't have known then that one day I would "swim for my life". My gratitude to him is beyond words and he would have been proud to be part of my survival attempt.

Now my fate was in my own hands, and as I swam my

mind was made up, I had to get across and live to tell the tale. Whether anyone would believe this tale was not uppermost in my thoughts at this moment and I carried on with the old-fashion over-arm stroke, which was not elegant but did the job.

Fitness was not a problem as I had trained regularly for two years and I swam quite strongly until I was about halfway across when I started to slow down. I floated on my back using a light paddling movement to keep me afloat, then once more forcing arms and legs to drive me on.

I felt I had been in the water for hours and with my head just clear I stared at the far bank still some considerable distance away.

When you are halfway across a river nearly a mile wide there is not a lot of choice, it was just as far to go back as it was to go forward, a bit Irish but it was a fact.

The sun was now overhead beating down on me but the water was keeping me cool and on any other day in different circumstances could have been a pleasant swim, but this was a survival swim.

I had been driven to this ordeal as an alternative to being killed or at best being taken prisoner and facing a living hell in the hands of sadistic yellow men.

An American correspondent writing about the war in later years stated that "in places, the river was a mile and a half wide"; I cannot confirm this but I would not disagree with his conclusion.

There was no one swimming near me and I knew if I panicked it was all over, so gathering all my strength I forced my tiring arms and legs to keep going.

Not many people would like to find themselves in this situation and it was touch and go whether I would soon drown, but I had to think positively, I felt I was too young to die and if I survived there was a wonderful world out there that I could enjoy.

Gradually the far bank was getting closer, about a hundred yards from safety I was overcome with fatigue and my limbs were tired and not giving me the strength I needed for a final push to the west bank.

Now I was slipping down into the river. Why I didn't panic and thrash around to keep my head above water I shall never know; perhaps when the end is near we have to accept our fate and my luck was surely running out.

But I was perfectly calm and slowly went deeper with the water gradually covering my face. In a matter of seconds I should not be able to breath and water would fill my lungs.

Would my epitaph be "drowned while trying to escape from the enemy on February 23rd 1942, aged 21"? It was in the lap of the Gods, but it was not to be...this day was not to be my last.

The soles of my feet touched something sandy. I had sunk down on to a sandbank, perhaps a hundred to one chance, but I gratefully accepted it.

With astonishment and great relief, I stayed motionless, and then moving my arms I waited for some energy to surge back into my aching limbs.

The short distance to the bank was swum in good time, and I flopped down on the bank in the warm sunshine, happy to be alive.

Against all the odds I had conquered this mighty river. Many of the 17th Division had drowned in their attempt to escape. Among them were friends I had known for the last two years and it was only much later that I realised the impact this tragedy would have on their families and friends.

Those of us who made it by boat, raft, or by swimming across the river, now swollen to one and half miles by the incoming tide, owed a great deal to the covering forces who held off the Japanese throughout that long, hot and thirsty day.

These troops put their lives in danger so that hundreds of us could make our escape. OK, not all of us were successful but those who were probably owed thier lives to these brave men.

In the jungle the Japs had complete moral ascendancy. It required two long years of training before the British and Indian armies were able to wrest it from them. Perhaps it was the feeling of isolation, which was so frightening. Where were the enemy? What would happen if you were wounded? Who would know? Panic was never far from the surface. The slightest rustle led to prickles all over, trigger fingers became itchy.

Up to now the Japs were having it all their own way, as they continuously smashed our defensive positions. They greedily took the supplies that we were forced to leave behind and must have thought that Christmas had come early, that's if they celebrated it.

So Far So Good

In contrast to the east bank the thick tropical jungle was no more, for now we were fighting in the dry belt of Burma where the rainfall is comparatively light. Everywhere it was parched and brown, cut by chaungs running into the rivers and lying across our line of retreat. A chaung is a watercourse and at this time of year they were mostly dry. Heat was intense for this was the hot season with temperatures running up to 110 degrees in the shade and there was little shade and often agonising thirst, for water was a rare and most precious commodity.

I badly needed help from any of our troops, who might have been on the lookout for anyone who had made the crossing, but I was out of luck, there was no sign of anyone and I shouted out, more in desperation than hope.

Although I was used to the heat, the tropical sun beating down on my near naked body was not an ideal situation.

Having got this far there was only one thing to do and that was to get away from this river as fast as I could and find what was left of my Battalion.

What I wouldn't have given for the boots that I had dumped on the other side of the river as bare-footed I covered several miles of countryside before I was faced with my next obstacle.

A short distance to my left was a solitary small bamboo hut and curiosity got the better of me as I wandered over to take a look at it. I should have remembered the old saying: "never look for trouble".

From behind the hut a dark skinned Burmese man appeared, probably wondering what this near naked white man was doing on his territory. He did not speak, but the look on his face made me feel uneasy.

One hand was held behind his back and when he brought it forward a lethal looking knife flashed in the sun.

In my few days in action I had been machine gunned by Jap fighters, fired at and mortared by fanatical yellow soldiers, miraculously crossed a near mile wide fast flowing Burmese river; now discretion had to be the better part of valour.

Wearing just a pair of shorts I was no match for this evil looking man. Had I moved any closer to him that knife would surely have fatally wounded me. I had always been a good runner and barefoot or not I turned away and ran as fast as I could.

If I had been carrying my bayonet I may have considered standing my ground as I was quite capable of looking after myself but this was a bit too one-sided for my liking.

Glancing back I was extremely thankful that he had not decided to give chase, although he was staring menacingly after me.

The distance between us increased rapidly and breathing heavily I slowed down and once more gazed ahead into the distance and contemplated what "thrills" fate still had in store for me.

From the time I entered the river early in the morning, apart from the Corporal who quickly left me I had no support whatsoever and it was a strain to have to make all my own decisions.

In the distance enemy planes were circling round ready to swoop on any of our lads caught in the open, but they did not seem interested in a lone near naked soldier making his way to safety, he hoped.

Feeling the intense heat and desperately in need of a drink I approached a village, which I later learned was called Abya, and was eight miles from the river, comprising numerous bamboo huts on stilts in case of flooding.

Most of us are not used to walking bare footed, except perhaps around the house, can you imagine what it was like to walk and run, with no protection for your feet, for eight miles across rough country.

I had no choice but to press on and blackout the pain and blisters, but believe me it took some doing.

I was extremely vulnerable now. The Japs could be anywhere, Burmese had murdered my Colonel and I was absolutely defenceless should I be attacked.

Some villagers approached me wondering no doubt what this crazy white man, completely alone, wearing only a pair of shorts, under a blazing hot sun was doing there.

As we were to quickly learn all Burmese were not pro British and a dead soldier would be a bonus for the villagers when the Japanese arrived.

They gestured to me to go into their village and through a crowd that had gathered an important looking Burmese man came up to me.

He spoke reasonably good English and I endeavoured to explain to him how I had got into this predicament.

He seemed very concerned as to who had destroyed their wonderful bridge and who could blame him when this could affect their means of transport and a lifeline for their very existence. But this was not my fault and I had to present a plausible explanation or I could be in deep trouble.

Choosing my words very carefully, I told him that the Burma Army had blown the bridge to stop the Japanese pouring into their country and committing indescribable atrocities to his people.

I told him I had swum the river to escape death or imprisonment and that our troops would be searching for stragglers and would thank the villagers for helping me. He thought hard and long, but seemed satisfied with this statement and thankfully for me he smiled.

I wish to pause here and make a statement to the reader of my wartime escapade who feels that this is becoming a fantasy of my imagination. Let me assure you that every word I have written, although it is sixty years later, is an accurate account, as far as I remember, about the events prior to and after the battle at the River Sittang.

Most factual war books I have read are based on interviews by the author of people who were involved in some way or another during the war, whether army, airforce, navy or civilian and not necessarily the exploits of the author. I feel that my book is mainly my own story and probably therefore more interesting for the reader than just interviewing people.

With that off my chest I will continue.

The next thing that happened was that the Headman spoke to some of the villagers in Burmese and they quickly disappeared from the crowd that had surrounded me.

The men who had been sent away now returned with wide grins on their faces. Hey presto – a shirt well worn, but very essential, was thrust towards me, followed by a skirt, which was traditional dress, a pair of slipper type shoes and a turban made out of a scarf.

I put on the clothes and shoes much to the amusement of the assembled audience. I didn't feel embarrassed but pleased to be covered up.

What a pity someone didn't have a camera so I could pose in my new outfit, which would have caused some amusement when showing my family and friends in later years.

Now protected from the shimmering heat I was able to continue my trek to safety and as my feet were covered I felt much more comfortable and almost pain free.

From a distance I could have been taken for a native of the country and to complete the picture, in case the enemy spotted me I rubbed dirt on my face and legs. With a final gift of Cheroots the villagers pointed me in the direction I had to take.

I wonder if some of the villagers tell their grandchildren of the day a white man, dressed only in a pair of shorts, arrived at their village, after swimming the mighty Sittang.

They had been very kind and generous to me and it was a pity I couldn't reward them, but that was not possible.

The town of Pegu where the army was assembling was my target, but this was over twenty miles away so without divine intervention I was going to struggle to make it.

Having covered the ground in good time, now that I was protected from the heat, I approached the outskirts of a large village and wandered aimlessly between the bamboo huts.

Out of the blue, someone called to me in English, inviting me into their hut. My disguise was obviously not a hundred percent and someone had spotted the pretence.

A young man helped me climb the ladder to get into his stilted hut, he told me he had been a student in Rangoon University when the Japanese invaded Burma and decided that his village would be a safer place to be.

We talked for some time over a welcome cup of tea and he seemed very interested when I recalled my experiences over the previous few days which now seemed some time ago.

He left the bamboo hut and I was alone in a sparsely furnished room, but it was clean and the mats we sat on were reasonably comfortable.

After about half an hour he returned and asked me to look outside. There was a cart filled with straw and a mule in its shafts.

This young Burmese student was so concerned for me to reach the troops now assembling a few miles away in Pegu that he put his own life at risk by organising this means of escape.

Climbing into the cart, watched with great curiosity by a small crowd of onlookers who couldn't quite understand what was taking place I covered myself with straw and the driver trundled along the track towards Pegu.

Whether or not the driver realised the danger he was placing himself in I don't know, he was either a hero or an idiot because if the Japs had suddenly arrived and found me they wouldn't have thought twice about running their bayonets through him.

This was like something out of a film, hidden in this cart, while the driver urged his mule along at a very steady pace, very hot, me dressed as a Burmese, I didn't know which way we were going, what if I was been taken to the Japanese, I could have been shot on the spot as a spy for being in disguise.

Without the help of the villagers and the student it is possible that I wouldn't have made it from the river to Pegu considering the distance, heat, lack of protection and the need of some liquid.

Several hours later, after being bumped up and down on the wooden floor, I heard voices that were definitely British.

In a flash I was out of the cart, explaining to some soldiers who I was and which Battalion I was with, they laughed and directed me to a hut where an officer listened to this explanation I gave him for being in the disguise of a Burmese.

He shook my hand and congratulated me on my determination and enterprise to get back to my Battalion.

Whether in the long run I would get out of Burma I didn't care, I was alive and for the time being safe.

I would have liked to thank all the Burmese that had helped me to escape but it was impossible and my only hope was that they survived the war.

Recently my daughter and her husband visited the Bridge over the River Kwai and brought back these pictures. It is now steel and stone construction but the bridge built by prisoners of war was made of wood collected from the surrounding jungle. Had I been taken prisoner I could have been involved in this as many of my mates probably were. How many of them were buried in the many cemeteries, having died as a result of working on the railway, I don't know but it was a cruel way to end their lives.

After the Sittang Battle

By begging or stealing the Quartermaster's staff appropriated uniforms, underclothes and boots to make us look like soldiers again. The only hats they could get hold of were Australian Bush Hats, which we soon wore with pride.

All through the night of February 23rd and throughout the 24th, 25th and 26th men of 17 Division staggered into Pegu, single as I had, in two's and three's and parties of twenty or thirty.

These were not all soldiers in uniform because the majority had got across the river by swimming or any means possible.

Clothes were at a premium, most men were practically naked and parts of Pegu were more like a nudist colony than a military camp, but the lads were in good spirits and laughed and joked with each other, happy to be alive and were more interested in obtaining food and drink than clothes. Luckily it was hot, so clothing was not so essential for survival providing the tropical sun didn't burn you.

For the time being I kept my Burmese clothing on and I seemed to be the only one in this disguise. I noticed a few funny looks in my direction, which was not surprising.

B Company of the 2nd Battalion Duke of Wellingtons, who had been in action on the east side of the Bridge when it was blown, had been given up for lost but they marched far to the north of the Bridge and eventually crossed on a ferry which was being run by friendly Burmese.

On the evening of February 24th, the counting of heads in the shattered 17th Division started and the figures made grim reading. When it seemed that all who could come in had done so, it was found that of twelve original battalions of infantry there now remained only 80 British officers, 69 Indian and Gurkha officers and 3335 other ranks, this represented a deficiency of approximately 5000. Their armaments totalled 1420 rifles, 56 light machine guns – a loss of 6000 weapons.

My Battalion, 2nd Duke of Wellingtons, waited for all the stragglers to arrive before making a final count. There were about 400 officers and men out of a total of 600 who had gone into action just a few days before.

So the reality was that approximately 200 officers and men had been killed, drowned or taken prisoner. A third of our Battalion lost, mainly due to the Sittang Bridge being blown up with most of us on the wrong side of the river.

General Smyth was blamed for the bridge decision and was relieved of his command by General Wavell who was Commander-in-Chief of the Burma Army. General Smyth had pleaded with Wavell some days before the bridge was blown to allow him to withdraw all of his Division immediately across the bridge and set up a defensive position on the open space that was available on the west side. Wavell would not even consider Smyth's plans and dismissed them without a second thought.

I felt sorry for General Smyth because he was in a no win situation and had to obey orders from his senior officers knowing that he would be accused of the tragic loss of life because of the decision to blow the bridge.

Later on I heard stories, some tragic, some amusing, of

how officers and men had put their lives in danger by helping wounded and non-swimmers to get across the river.

One young soldier of the "Dukes" with a grin on his face told me that he had asked his sergeant: "what'll we do now Sarge?" "Swim for it," said the sergeant. "But I can't swim Sarge". The immediate reply was "you'll soon have a chance to learn."

Six Gurkha riflemen, who could not swim, found a large log, in size and shape resembling a telegraph pole. The Gurkhas lifted the log bodily and heaved it into the water. Under the critical eye of their Havildar they adjusted their Gurkha hats and slung their rifles on their backs. They then straddled the log and using pieces of wood as paddles set off for the West bank with Havildar Sherbahadur shouting the time like a cox in the Boat race.

Men in the water had little breath for cheering, and indeed there was little to cheer about, but men in the immediate vicinity roared encouragement as the Gurkhas sped past them determined to reach the other side at all costs.

The odds against their reaching safely must have been enormous, but we like to think that these great little warriors reached the end of their perilous voyage without disaster.

A soldier that I spoke to later told me he had multiple splinter wounds and on reaching the river made a raft from some bits of wood and fishing nets. With five non-swimmers holding on, he pushed it across to the far bank. On landing he was in a bad way, very weak and tottery. Someone produced a bottle of beer from goodness knows where which they gave to the soldier who opened it with his teeth and then, on the contents, walked twenty-five miles in bare feet.

Major Harvey-Williams, of the 3/7th Gurkhas, eyed the Sittang with the gravest misgivings, swimming had never been a hobby of his and he had a bullet in his right arm.

With him were several of his men and death by drowning was clearly uppermost in their minds, but they looked at Harvey-Williams with calm confidence – the major sahib would think of something, but how would he get them out of this mess?

No, they answered in unison to the Major's first question, they could not swim, strange that the majority of Gurkhas were non-swimmers, but they had no intention of being captured by the enemy.

There were petrol cans nearby and Harvey-Williams quickly realised that they would float in the river, so he gave his men their survival instructions: "tie the petrol cans to your chests with puttees, get in the water and kick with your feet and hope for the best".

It was the only solution he could come up with in the desperate circumstances, for at least they had two good arms, but he was faced with making the crossing with one good arm.

After the first hundred yards, it was painfully apparent to him that he was not going to reach the far bank unless some miracle intervened. At that moment a large log floated past and he managed to hook his good arm over it.

But he had overtaxed his strength on the journey so far, his wounded arm throbbed abominably and he barely had sufficient strength in the other to hold on. Clinging on for dear life his legs trailing helplessly, he and the log were swept downstream.

Considerably more dead than alive, Major Harvey-Williams eventually reached the west bank two hours later and two miles farther down the river.

Another incident, which took place at the River Sittang, concerned three "Dukes", Major Robinson, Corporal Fox and Lance-Corporal Roebuck. On arrival at the river the

Major took responsibility for approximately 300 troops.

As well as Major Robinson's decimated "Dukes" C Company there were Gurkhas and Indians who were unbelievably non-swimmers.

When the bridge was blown the Japs moved farther north to find another crossing. Apart from the odd sniper bullets, Robinson decided he could take a chance, and moved his troops to the mangled remains of the bridge.

What he quickly realised was that his troops could climb along the girders that still remained either side of the river. What he had to provide was a lifeline to stretch between what girders remained and the 300 yards of fast flowing tidal water. There was not enough rope for this purpose and Major Robinson with his two volunteers, Corporal Fox and Lance-Corporal Roebuck, soon swam across the river, as they were all excellent swimmers.

They returned with several lengths of rope, which they knotted, together to the remaining girders to form a lifeline. They remained in the water while something like 300 men crossed the river to safety.

Major Robinson was awarded the Military Cross and Fox and Roebuck were decorated with Military Medals.

Another of the many river stories that I heard of was that of CQMS H. Darby who swam the river to the west bank in order to find a boat, he found one and plugged the hole in the bottom and paddled it back to the other side. He lifted an injured Captain Howden into the boat and several other wounded and non-swimmers also got in and the boat was pushed off. About fifteen yards from the near shore it sank. Captain Howden swam back to the shore; a more desperate and agonising effort with his shattered leg it would be hard to imagine. Then with the non-swimmers hanging on, Howden baling out with his hat and Darby paddling the boat, the party set off again and eventually reached the other side. Howden was placed on a door and carried along the railway line until an engine was found. He was dumped on top of the coal in the tender and taken to Wah. He induced someone to put him on a refugee train and three days later arrived at Mandalay with his wound still undressed. Gangrene had set in and amputation of his leg was necessary, such were the chaotic conditions behind the lines.

So those of us who were not drowned, shot in the water by snipers or strafed by marauding dive-bombers came to the west bank of the Sittang.

Jaded spirits were somewhat raised on February 26th when "C" Company of the Cameroonians made 220 dixies of tea for stragglers still coming in after the Sittang crossing, and if this seems a trivial remark in a story about a historic retreat never let us underestimate the value of tea.

Fighting Our Way Out of Pegu

The 2nd Battalion Duke of Wellingtons having lost a third of its troops was formed into a new Battalion as a temporary measure with the 2nd Kings Own Yorkshire Light Infantry (2nd KOYLI) who had also lost a big proportion of their Battalion and became known as "The Kings Own Dukes".

My Battalion had been wrecked by the tragedy of the Sittang Bridge. Many of the experienced officers, warrant officers and NCOs had been killed or were in hospital with wounds or illness and there were few men left. Clothing was in tatters; many of those left had no boots and very little weapons or equipment. During the first few days at Pegu it did not seem possible that my Battalion could be revived to take any further part in this bloody war.

After the disaster that had befallen 17 Division the Japs did not immediately follow up their success and provided us with precious breathing space, which we used to form ourselves into a fighting force in Pegu.

The Royal Ordnance Corps had the unenviable task of supplying the Division with weapons, vehicles and ammunition. It was not far short of a miracle that they could even supply a portion of our demands and deserved a big thank you for their effort.

Mountain Battery on the move

It should be realised that, throughout this part of the campaign, casualties were always liable to occur, and frequently did so, from attacks by Burmans. The people of the plains of Burma like to be on the winning side, as the Japanese were to find out to their cost in 1945. In 1942, although about 90 per cent were either neutral or friendly to the British, the other 10 per cent caused much trouble to the fighting and administrative troops. There were roving bands of armed Burmans, frequently officered by Japanese, and there were dacoits whose sole aim was to get as much as possible for themselves while the opportunity lasted.

We were safe for the time being but it could only be a brief pause before the Japanese Division who was still at full strength would move in and surround us.

We had little hope of holding any part of Burma against the victorious Japanese and yet there were only two ways out of the country. We could follow the mountain road to Chungking in China from Mandalay and Lashio or we could attempt to cross the mountains into India. Work had begun to drive a road through the mountains and this went on night and day in a desperate bid to save the lives of us soldiers.

Help was on its way, but the ordinary soldiers were not aware of any reinforcements until they were told later.

Some 50 miles south of Pegu was the large port of Rangoon, which was heavily bombed, but continued to function long enough to get troops and tanks unloaded and assembled.

Air raids, in which anti-personnel bombs had been used with terrible effect on the unsuspecting population, had utterly disorganised Rangoon. More than half a million Indians had started their flight to India, a march that was to end in death for many tens of thousands.

When the "Honey" tanks of the 7th Hussars eventually appeared in Pegu we were completely stunned and shocked. The sound of metal tracks coming up the road made us jump up and down with excitement, these tanks would fight side by side with us and give us a chance to escape the steel band the Japs had put round us.

I felt happier that I was now back with my Battalion and with some of the other lads I dug trenches, checked ammunition, and in the evenings we wandered over to the 7th Brigade headquarters and listened to their radios when they played forces music including Vera Lynne's, "We'll meet again". I wonder!

At this time of the year the brilliant tropical sun shines down all day and every day, very hot in the middle of the day; the nights are clear, starlit and fairly cool, noisy with myriads of insects, bats and nocturnal birds.

General Alexander was appointed by Churchill to command the Burma Army and he moved up from Rangoon with the reinforcements having decided that the port could not be defended, but not before the oil installations and anything that would be of use to the enemy was completely destroyed.

The Armoured Brigade, with the Cameroonians and West Yorks, moved out from Rangoon heading for Pegu to strengthen the shattered 17th Division.

Between Rangoon and Pegu the Japs set up another of their trump cards, a roadblock, at a place called Taukkyan,

These road blocks might at first consist of only a few men concealed at the edge of the road; later it might be developed into a strongly held position with felled trees and overturned lorries on the road.

About 100 tanks were moving north supported by several thousand troops the Japs placed a tree across the road and as the leading tank slowed down it received a direct hit which killed all the crew.

The tanks and infantry immediately went into action and fought hard to break the block, eventually; through sheer tenacity and courage they cleared the road and carried on to Pegu.

The Taukkyan roadblock was not intended to trap Alexander; it was part of a broader plan to take Rangoon by surprise; the port could be seized without first having to overcome the forces, which stood in their way.

General Sakurai, commanding the Japanese 33rd Division, wanted Rangoon for the port facilities and the oil. His troops viewed the imminent capture of Rangoon with pleasurable anticipation and opportunities for loot and rape on a grand scale.

There was nothing triumphal about the Japanese entry into

Rangoon at midday on March 8th; there was no oil refinery and no port facilities worthy of the name.

Nothing to rape and little to loot, the departing population had seen to that. There were only fires and the smell of death and decay, the human population was reduced to the dead and the dying.

The situation would have been worse had not the Governor set in motion Stage Two of the Rangoon Evacuation Scheme, There was an immediate panic. The police virtually collapsed. People fought to get on trains, or travelled on cars, bullock carts, bicycles, tricycles and anything else that moved. Men, women and children sat on carriage roofs, clung on to buffers and outside carriage windows, sat on top of each other inside the carriages and fought with knives to gain a footing.

How desperate were these poor people to escape from Japanese occupation. Can you imagine shutting your front door, leaving all your possessions behind, not knowing if you would ever occupy your house again and would you even be alive to return?

Lunatics were turned loose from the asylum. Wild animals escaped from the zoo, criminals were released from the jails, and chaos reigned for days on end.

Now gathered altogether in Pegu the reorganised 17th Division, supported by the 7th Armoured Brigade, 1st West Yorkshires, and 1st Cameroonians, were gearing up for the fight of their lives for they were now surrounded by battle hardened Jap troops ready to use their artillery, mortars and tanks to overcome any resistance we could throw at them.

There were only two roads out of Pegu suitable for our tanks and vehicles and the Jap technique of roadblocks would lead to some fierce fighting if we were to move up country towards India and safety.

The "Dukes" were allocated three Armoured Carriers,

which had been shipped in from the Desert. They were armour-plated but completely open at the top, probably alright for the open Desert, but as we soon found out not sufficient protection travelling on a road with jungle either side.

A grenade or mortar lobbed in would kill all the crew in one go, but we were not allowed to voice our opinion on the subject and as was expected in the British Army we obeyed orders and got on with the job.

I was part of the crew of one of these Carriers, which had a total of four; commander, driver and two others with Bren guns, rifles and grenades.

We went out on several patrols, mostly at night, it was eerie travelling through the pitch-black countryside.

One night we were sent miles towards the river to search for some Burmese officials who had crossed the river by some means or other and wanted to escape from the Japanese.

Captain Christison was in charge of our Carriers and as we sped through the darkness I gripped my Bren gun and made sure I had some grenades handy ready for any eventuality.

We stopped near a village and dismounted, moving forward listening for any sign of the enemy.

There was a deadly silence, which could be broken at any time if we were spotted, but the officials had not arrived and after waiting for some hours our leader decided to start back and maybe try another day.

As we travelled back to Pegu one our Carriers skidded off the road and I ran to see if I could help the lads in any way.

They were not badly injured but shaken up and a bit dazed. The grenades that were loose in the Carrier were spread all over the floor and we were worried that if one went off it could set off the others and we should most likely be killed.

We helped the lads get out of the Carrier and sorted out the ammunition ready to carry on the return trip.

A few days later our three Armoured Carriers patrolled out of Pegu on the road leading to Prome.

On a hot sunny morning they made good speed along the road watching intently for any sign of the Japanese.

They were completely alone with no support on a dangerous mission that should not have been sanctioned in the first place as no one new exactly where the Japs were hiding

Without any warning they suddenly hit the dreaded roadblock, with the approach to the obstacle covered by anti-tank and machine gun fire, supported by infantry with mortars, they were utterly and completely out-gunned.

Captain John Christison who was in charge of the operation was in the leading Carrier. He and his crew never stood a chance when his Carrier took a direct hit, killing all the crew and blasting his Carrier off the road.

I had got to know John Christison very well on our scouting trips, although once more fate had intervened and I had not been detailed to ride in his Carrier.

I was very impressed by his gentlemanly manner, he was quietly spoken but very determined and I am sure he died doing his duty without any thought of safety for himself.

What I had dreaded had happened, with no protection for the Carrier apart from the sides, but my voice had not been heard.

By a strange coincidence, Captain John Christison's father, General Sir Philip Christison, was also serving in Burma when John, who was his only son, was killed.

General Christison must have been shattered when he received the tragic news and I as a private soldier felt very upset when I saw his Carrier smashed into the edge of the jungle.

At the end of the war General Christison took the submission of the Japanese Seventh Area Army and the South Seas Fleet, a moment of great personal significance, for it was his 15th Corps who had been the first to re-enter Rangoon.

I would like to have met this great General to tell him that his son had given his life carrying out his orders.

What a tragedy, four more "Dukes" killed, where would it all end and how many more would lose their lives before this carnage ended.

The two following Carriers, driven with reasonable space between them braked hard and backed up as fast as possible.

Their Bren guns fired back but they were ineffective against this force and with great daring our drivers turned and headed back to report the enemy position.

A Squadron of the 7th Hussars, in their "Honey" tanks, charged down the road full tilt at the road-block, smashing through with utter disregard for their own safety. The sound of metal tracks on the hard surface and the guns firing was something that will always stay in the memory of those privileged to watch.

In later years I was struck by a cruel twist of fate. General Christison's son John was killed in Burma in 1942 and General Smyth's son, also called John and a Captain, was killed in Northern Burma in 1945 when the war was nearly over. Two great Generals having to accept the same tragic circumstances.

This was not the final nail in the coffin and to continue this tragic sequence of events we must include General "Punch" Cowan who took command of 17 Division when General Smyth was relieved of his duties. His son joined the 1/6 Gurkhas, Cowans and Slims old regiment and died from his wounds in the assault on Mandalay towards the end of the war. Fate had been cruel to these three Generals, as they must have thought they had enough to get on with without this terrible news.

The fighting at Pegu, where most of the forces were dug in, was on a scale of savagery and confusion hitherto unencountered in the Burma campaign.

The troops defending Pegu were disposed as follows: 48th Gurkha Brigade covered the town from the east, the West Yorkshires covered the area north-west of the town; the Cameroonians were in Pegu itself, guarding the road bridges across the river and railway; the 7th Hussars were at the northern exit.

We were bombed from the air, shelled, mortared and machine-gunned incessantly. The battle had resolved itself into desperate last stands by units all mixed up – British, Indians, and Gurkhas fighting shoulder to shoulder together with the tanks of the 7th Armoured Brigade.

The Japanese had Pegu most thoroughly surrounded and General Alexander in desperation ordered all his troops to break out independently to the north.

We despaired of any good news and would have to fight on to survive being killed or taken prisoner.

To stop us breaking out of Pegu the Japs threw up a network of roadblocks at every exit.

With a ferocious tenacity the Gurkhas, with a blood-curdling scream, smashed through one of the first roadblocks on the road leading to Prome.

I don't know when the Gurkhas first started using their war cry but believe me when you hear it, it sends a shiver through you and you would not like to face these tough little warriors in full flight.

So it went on, leap-frogging, fighting, resting briefly, leap-frogging again, fighting off attacks from both flanks, jumping into ditches as the bombers and fighters came over, cursing the lack of any air support.

I was in one of our Carriers travelling along the road behind the tanks and not scared about what was happening all around me but looking up the road searching for the next roadblock that would not be far away.

At every road-block regardless of the risk, a squadron of the 7th Hussars was to hand, the officers standing up in their tanks, with turrets open, in much the same way as the horsed 7th Hussars had galloped into action at Waterloo.

Troopers leapt from their tanks, gathered up wounded and stragglers, loaded them on to the tanks and thundered on.

If it had not been for the tanks of the 7th Armoured Brigade we should never have fought our way out of Pegu.

So the survivors of the Sittang battle, and the reinforcements that had got in before Rangoon was captured, headed northward on the road to Prome with the burning heap of rubble that was now Pegu left far behind.

The lads that died were given a burial service of some kind if it was possible and the padres were being called on to do their duty if they were available, but they were human and could be in great danger themselves at times, what was certain was that none of the dead soldiers relatives would be present.

Burma Army Heads for Prome

As the Army withdrew along the Prome Road it resembled a mechanical, slow-crawling centipede. From front to rear it measured several miles. Thick clouds of dust rose in the air as the column of lorries, ambulances, Bren Carriers and tanks ground along a road never intended to take such a volume of traffic. Trudging alongside on the verges were lines of sweat-grimed soldiers who had little idea of what was going on or where they were heading. In the background burned the funeral pyre of Burma's greatest port, Rangoon.

General Wavell, Commander-in-Chief of the Burma Army, who was accountable to Prime Minister Churchill for the disasters in Malaya and Burma was desperate for some good news. He cabled his deputy, General Alexander: "understand from naval authorities decision taken to evacuate Rangoon, cable most immediate reasons for this very grave step which affects whole course of war in the Far East, has battle taken place?"

The new Commander's reply was blunt and forthright; the counter-attacks had failed with heavy losses and his main task now was to save his army from destruction and hold as much of Upper Burma as possible.

The defeats that we had sustained were due to two main causes, faulty tactical deployment of the British forces and inexperience of our troops. When it came to fighting, the British, Indian and Gurkha soldiers were every bit as good as the Japanese, but owing to the ability of the Japanese to concentrate silently and unseen in the jungle the scales were too heavily weighted against the Burma Army from the start.

The tropical nights closed in rapidly and the darkness was intense. The tiniest sound caused merely by the movement of an insect could also herald an attack by the enemy.

It wasn't long before the next inevitable roadblock was set up stopping the Burma Army in its tracks.

It couldn't be in a worse position, on one side of the road was dense jungle, on the other a rubber plantation, and from both sides unseen snipers were able to maintain a continuous and accurate fire on anything that moved.

If the Japanese Air Force had made a concentrated attack on the mass of tanks and vehicles halted on this single road a massive disaster would have taken place

There were only a few planes swooping down on the column, which were met by a hail of fire from small arms and Bren guns fired from the hip or resting on the backs of comrades.

Blocking the road was a tree trunk and some 40-gallon drums of highly inflammable oil and tar, speared to the ground with steel spikes. Almost immediately a tank, which went forward, to reconnoitre was hit and set on fire. Within an area of a square mile 17 Division with their reinforcements became bogged down in a bumper-to-bonnet jam of double-banked vehicles.

The tank crews, their backs bronzed from the desert sun calmly clambered out of their turrets to light cigarettes and brew tea. Gunners rested near their field and anti-tank guns.

Some moved off the road and deployed to battle positions. British soldiers, Gurkhas and Indians, worn out by days of fighting, slumped down by the roadside only too glad to ease their cramped and aching legs. To add to the confusion the Army was further hampered by the presence of thousands of refugees and countless civilian vehicles.

What a pitiful sight these refugees made, worried, hungry, thirsty, they plodded along the side of the road pleading with us to give them a lift, which we did when possible, but only a small proportion could be helped and the rest, carrying children and all their possessions on their heads and shoulders trudged on while the sun beat down remorselessly.

General Alexander, who was completely unflappable, sat in a camp chair, his head in his hands, helpless to do anything until the roadblock had been broken.

It seemed incredible that an entire Army could be halted in its tracks by such a primitive obstacle but such was the terrain that it was almost impossible to destroy the block with artillery fire, yet somehow or other it had to be forced.

The Gloucesters who were leading the column were informed by a senior Staff Officer that they had been given the task of breaking through.

The Staff Officer informed Colonel Bagot of the Gloucesters that he would have some artillery and tank support and it was merely a question of pushing up the road, as the enemy did not consist of more than a patrol, with that the Staff Officer disappeared.

Strategy that was used in the First World War when the senior officers ordered the troops in their thousands to "go over the top" and face a massacre had not altered as we were seeing every day in Burma where life was becoming a lottery. Colonel Bagot was joined by one of the tank commanders and an artillery officer and together they surveyed the block and the burning tank, which had been knocked out trying to break through.

Having studied the scene, the artillery officer explained that his 25-pounders could not smash the block, as the trees were too dense. A position might however be found some way back from which fire could be brought to bear on a small area, but the problem was that there was no observation post from which to study the effect. The tank commander was adamant that no more tanks should be endangered, the anti-tank guns would have to be knocked out and the roadblock cleared by infantry, then the tanks would follow.

Colonel Bagot with only one Company of the Gloucesters was faced with only one option; he would obey orders to smash the block knowing it would be a suicide attack.

He turned and shouted: "to hell with the tanks and artillery the Gloucesters are going forward and remember the Gloucesters don't know how to retreat".

B Company advanced with a platoon either side of the road and a third in reserve on the left. Enemy mortars and heavy machine gun fire was returned by the advancing Gloucesters. Two Bren Carriers were sent forward in support and Colonel Bagot clambered aboard the first carrier to lead the assault by his men.

The carriers raced up the narrow road and Japanese soldiers hiding in the undergrowth opened up on them with a barrage of small arms and mortars. The second carrier received a direct hit, which killed the entire crew.

Bagot speeded up and smashed into the block but in doing so damaged a track and slewed round at right angles, which brought the carrier to an abrupt halt.

B Company walked into a withering hail of machine gun and rifle fire while the platoon on the left was caught in an ambush and were completely encircled when only fifty yards from the block. Another platoon made a wide circling movement and almost reached the road obstacle when a large enemy group attacked it. The platoon advancing on the right side of the road also ran into heavy and devastating fire from well-concealed snipers.

Colonel Bagot and his driver slid into a ditch and managed to get back. Bagot ordered one platoon to advance again and try to secure the wood on the right, while another was sent to try and take the other side.

Because the losses had been so severe and there were no reserves available, a patrol was hastily made up which included signallers and stretcher-bearers to make a direct assault.

One enemy party opened fire at a range of less than twenty yards and the Gloucesters went in with the bayonet and the enemy broke and fled into the jungle. But fire immediately broke out on all sides and the Gloucesters realised too late that they had been led into an ambush. They hurled grenade after grenade at the unseen enemy, but the undergrowth was so dense that several hit branches and bounced back. But they still managed to kill a large number of Japs and after several sorties they retreated but by this time the small party of Gloucester's had been reduced to three men.

The Gloucesters had fought without respite for four and a half hours against an entire Japanese battalion. Against such superior odds there was nothing more Colonel Bagot and his men could do.

When darkness descended Bagot made his way back and reported personally to General Alexander.

Alexander, who was not to escape criticism for his handling of the situation, listened attentively to Bagot and decided to march a battalion of Gurkhas through the night round the flank on the west side and attack the block from behind at first light. They would be supported by two British Battalions who had been following behind the main column and who would mount a frontal attack, this time there would be artillery and tank support.

As daylight approached the guns of the 12th Mountain Battery pounded the roadblock.

When the barrage lifted, the tanks and troops smashed their way through the roadblock with great determination, they were through and the Japanese fled into the jungle.

This was a brilliant victory for the Burma Army although they were withdrawing; they had defeated the Japanese troops and were still alive to carry on the fight.

Alexander could not believe his good fortune and leapt into a staff car and roared off up the Prome road to regroup his staff.

Now the road was clear we took advantage of any transport we could get on and when possible gave a lift to some of the refugees who were strung out all along the road. They must have been very frightened to leave their homes behind and walk hundreds of miles to escape from the Japanese. They were desperate for food and water and only their hope of survival kept them going.

With hindsight, General Wavell realised that he had asked the impossible of the new Army Commander, General Alexander and signalled: "well done, responsibility for position in which you and your troops were placed is wholly mine and I congratulate you all on determination with which you have extricated yourselves. Much regret casualties."

The 2nd Battalion Duke of Wellingtons, my battalion, had in a couple of weeks lost 200 out of 600, one in three killed or captured or drowned, so I think that our regret was far greater than General Wavells.

One afternoon when we were relaxing at the side of the road, three Japanese fighter planes passed low overhead, they had probably been shooting up our lads and the refugees struggling along the road.

An Ack Ack unit, well concealed nearby, opened fire and shot down one of these planes.

We cheered like mad at this, to think that we were fighting back and inflicting real damage on the enemy.

But this was not the end, the other two pilots were out to get revenge, they swooped down on us letting fly with their machine guns.

We were in great danger of being killed so we dashed for the slit trenches that we had dug which gave us some protection but we were unlucky as they struck an ammunition dump and shells passed very close overhead, for a few minutes all hell was let loose and we breathed a sigh of relief when it was calm again.

The wounded were taken away but once more I had escaped injury and wondered when my date with destiny would take place.

GENERAL "BILL" SLIM ARRIVES

General 'Bill' Slim

Although General Alexander's army was grossly under strength in men and materials he was still expected to inflict a major defeat on the enemy, but no matter how hard and how valiantly his soldiers fought it seemed that they could not stem the Japanese advance.

General Alexander requested an additional Corp Commander needed to support his Burma campaign. The man chosen by General Wavell to fill this role was Lieutenant-General William Slim. No Commander could have asked for a better or more reliable deputy.

Slim was a "soldier's soldier" in every sense of the word. He had enlisted as a Private, been made up to Lance-Corporal, and "busted" back to Private, been discharged as medically unfit after being badly wounded, yet somehow or other had rejoined and won an MC and DSO as a young officer in the First World War.

Slim's command was the newly formed Burcorps which consisted of the 17th Division under General "Punch" Cowan, the 1st Burma Division under Major-General Bruce Scott and the 7th Armoured Brigade under Brigadier John Anstice.

General Cowan was ordered to mount a counter-attack with his 17th Division. He decided to do so with a striking force consisting of one battery of artillery, tanks and three infantry battalions, the Gloucesters, the Duke of Wellingtons and the Cameroonians.

The counterattack achieved little but to add to the long list of casualties, 10 valuable tanks were lost and nearly 400 officers and men killed or wounded.

We did all we could and inflicted enormous losses on the enemy, but a withdrawal was inevitable and the tanks once more roared to the rescue bringing out the infantry, many of whom were badly wounded.

The battle south of Prome was a disaster for remnants of the 2nd Battalion Duke of Wellingtons. We lost five officers and 117 Other Ranks; so far in this Burma campaign we had lost nearly 400 out of an original battalion of 600.

Very few of those who were taken prisoner survived the inhumane treatment they endured in nearly four years of captivity.

Thousands of troops died when building the Burma railway under atrocious conditions with little food or drink to sustain their skinny bodies.

On reflection I believe I was extremely lucky to have survived the ordeal we were put through and this was not the end, I still had nearly a thousand miles to cover to get to Assam and safety.

The intense heat that I coped with fairly well coupled with the danger of attack from the air, meant that almost all movement had to be carried out by night, but this did not mean that the daylight hours could be devoted entirely to rest. Slit trenches had to be dug to give us protection from air attacks, water had to be fetched, sometimes from a considerable distance; animals and men had to be fed; patrolling carried out and foraging parties sent to purchase supplies.

Sometimes on our travels we passed houses or bungalows that the occupants had fled from. Curiosity got the better of us and occasionally we went in to their homes and had a look around. It was really sad to see the lovely condition of most of these places and although we could have taken anything we wanted, and there were valuable objects lying around, it was of no use to us. What a terrible state of affairs that the owners were so frightened for their lives that they left everything they possessed.

Of course the Burmese people stayed where they were, because it was their country, but the families who were Indian and mixed races did not trust the Japanese and left in great haste.

As we withdrew from the battle thirty miles south of Prome we received another setback.

Brigadier Anstice, commanding the 7th Armoured Brigade, was told that the town of Shwedaung on the main road ten miles south of Prome was in the hands of the enemy.

General Cowan ordered him to withdraw but this was easier said than done, for the Japanese had set up a series of roadblocks.

Roadblocks were a curse in the Burma campaign, with mostly jungle either side of a single road it was too easy for the enemy to move in under cover of darkness and completely stop us in our tracks.

There was no alternative, the roadblocks would have to be smashed and Brigadier Anstice ordered his advance guard to storm the southern end while the infantry attacked the northern end.

The men who had fought in the battle 30 miles south of Prome marched hard and long under a pitiless sun to reach the new roadblock, 10 miles south of Prome, but when they were ordered to try and dislodge the enemy there was no hesitation.

A Battery of 25 pounders hammered at the block for 15 minutes before the assault was launched. The fighting was again at close quarters and was so confusing that it was impossible to know where the firing was coming from. I decided, as I had done many times before, that the closer you could get to the ground the better the chance of surviving the bullets coming from the front and the ones coming from the rear.

Enemy snipers seemed to be concealed in every tree and house and cunningly sited machine guns and mortars were in every bamboo grove.

As tragedy followed tragedy one platoon of the "Dukes" lost all its five NCOs in the same number of minutes.

Communications being almost non-existent the relatives of the troops had no idea of the carnage that was taking place in this country where we were fighting for our lives.

One morning our Company was ordered to advance across some fields where the Japs were threatening to move in to put up a roadblock.

As they attacked us we hit the ground and let fly with everything we had, this didn't stop them and we were in danger of being shot up unless we made something happen quickly.

In battles heroes are made from normally placid individuals who suddenly take things into their own hands.

Suddenly something happened which those present would never forget.

For no understandable reason one of our lads who was carrying a machine gun stood up and fired a full magazine at the leading Japanese troops who were stopped in their tracks, completely shocked by this action.

They recovered and in a matter of seconds had killed him, but his example was enough to force us into action and we charged forward and routed them.

He received a medal for his gallantry but we shall never know what drove him to give his life for his country.

This war was not like any other. In the First World War the opposing sides faced each other and their lines of communication were kept intact, but now we were fighting to withdraw to a position where we could face the enemy the right way round.

Brigadier Anstice was desperate to break through and he decided to launch a night attack on the roadblock by tanks supported by artillery, a task that would have been almost impossible in daylight.

As the tanks roared forward at 35 miles an hour machine-gun bullets struck them and it was like hammer blows on the armour.

The battle lasted all night before the tanks and troops broke through but at a high cost. Hussars had lost 10 tanks, the artillery two guns and infantry 350 men killed or wounded.

About this time I was struck down with a dose of dysentery, which is not only weakening but also most inconvenient when you have to dive into the jungle at a minutes notice. We didn't have any medicine to counteract this and I was very unhappy while it lasted.

Without reinforcements or air support the task of holding Burma was becoming harder by the day and only a miracle would save more lives being lost. Not forgetting the refugees who were dying on the roadside in their hundreds owing to lack of medication and food. The majority were Indian, but there were also Anglo-Indians, Anglo-Burmans, Chinese, Burmese and some Europeans.

The Chinese were worried at the rapid advance of the Japanese through Burma, which bordered China, they would be vulnerable should the enemy continue its present rapid advance.

They sent their 200th Division to hold Toungoo where they fought with a fanaticism that was equal to that of the enemy, but outnumbered by at least three to one the outcome was inevitable.

When Toungoo finally fell General Slim considered it a disaster second only to the blowing up of the Sittang Bridge.

Having weighed up the situation "Slim" had to consider whether it was worth trying to hold Prome.

Little remained of the town, cholera was rife among refugees and spreading to the troops, stores urgently needed by the Army were piled up on the quays by the riverside. Plans were quickly made to backload supplies but as there was no railway out of Prome it had to be moved by boat.

General Slim who was as tough as they come, had been thrown into the middle of a war where the odds were against him from the start, he couldn't win, his job was to save as many lives as possible, mine included, with only the forces available in Burma.

Lieutenant-General T.J. Hutton

With the enemy so close he moved his headquarters thirty miles north to Allanmyo. Generals Wavell and Alexander visited him there and they quickly decided to begin the evacuation at once.

The great worry on their shoulders was how they could defend the oilfields at Yenangyaung on which the army now depended to keep their tanks and vehicles moving.

Slim realised that the situation was indeed grim. The 17th Division, which had been fighting without a pause since the start of the campaign, was in poor shape to repulse a strong and determined attack.

But the withdrawal plan became somewhat academic; it was the enemy who decided the fate of Prome by attacking in great strength before the plans to retreat could be activated.

An Indian Battalion lined up at the south end of the town and successfully repulsed the first attack on the night of 1-2 April.

This was a minor setback for the Japs and they infiltrated into the town in large numbers.

The ensuing battle was fierce and confusing and 17th Division was forced to retire to the north of the town. The tough little Gurkhas were loath to admit defeat and they set up an ambush where they slaughtered some two hundred of the enemy, holding their fire until they were only a few yards away.

The enemy were creating confusion and chaos with a series of devastating mortar and artillery barrages and there was a grave danger of the withdrawal becoming a disorderly rout.

It was imperative for 17 Division to move north as quickly as possible, for General Cowan dreaded another road-block which his exhausted troops would have great difficulty breaking through so he sent the tanks roaring to the rescue and two squadrons of the 2nd Royal Tank Regiment began ferrying the battle weary men back from Prome.

For eight hours the tanks ran a shuttle service and moved some 2500 troops. Although riding on tanks was about the most uncomfortable method of travelling ever devised these tank men had proved fine comrades in battle. The 2nd Royal Tank Regiment and the 7th Hussars had come straight from the Western Desert of Egypt to Rangoon and some of their tanks were still going when they at last reached northern Burma. There they destroyed them and the rusty shells stand as mementoes of a very fine effort.

In a message to General Wavell, Alexander stated that morale among his troops was not as high as it should be, they had been fighting continuously for three months and units were getting weaker and weaker, they had not received any reinforcements and had been bombed and machine-gunned with no hope of any air support.

General Wavell, Commander-in-Chief of the Far East forces, who was still thinking in 1914-18 terms, probably after much thought over a gin and tonic in his safe haven in India replied: "don't let the troops get too disheartened over the enemy's air superiority, it is nothing like so dangerous that we so frequently were up against in the last war".

Leland Stowe, an American war correspondent, told his American readers: "bravery was not enough, the British soldiers and the Indian troops in Burma fought with great courage whenever their leaders gave them the opportunity to fight. They did not fear to die and they were worthy of the finest and best in Britain and India's military tradition. When they lost confidence in their commanders it was only after most soldiers would have lost all faith".

I took each day as it came, wondering if someone up there was watching over me, for I had escaped death and injury so many times that a cat's nine lives had nothing on me.

KOYLI fought a brilliant action at Myingun, which saved the Burma Army from being cut off. When the news reached London, the Queen sent a personal message by wireless: "Commander-in-Chief is requested to convey the following message from Her Majesty the Queen to the Officer Commanding 2nd Battalion KOYLI. As your Colonel in Chief I have learned with pride of your splendid fight in recent days.

You are all much in my thoughts and I send my best wishes to all ranks".

The effect of such a message can well be imagined. But it was not received by the KOYLI. For in the chaos of the retreat and the breakdown of communication with India the message was never delivered. So the men fighting the long and apparently hopeless rearguard up the whole length of Burma never heard of their Queen's personal pride in their achievement.

The Oil Wells of Yenangyaung

The town and oil wells of Yenangyaung sprawled untidily over fifteen square miles on the banks of the Irrawaddy.

Thousands of steel derricks resembled a man-made forest, but was one of the richest areas in the world. It boasted 5000 oil wells, three petrol refineries and the largest power station in the whole of Burma.

What a magnificent vast fete of engineering to erect these oil wells in order to extract the oil that the world depended on to keep its transport and industry going.

The oilmen and their families lived in beautiful bungalows and the clubs were among the best in the country.

We had moved north to Yenangyaung outskirts and one day I was in an armoured carrier, which went on a scouting mission to the oilfields.

We drove along a narrow road watching intently for any sign of the enemy and I gripped my Bren gun ready to fire when the enemy appeared.

The countryside we travelled through was open and really lovely if you were interested in that sort of thing but our object was to stay alive and report back any troop movements in this area.

We went as close to the oilfields as we thought safe and stopped and surveyed the scene around us.

Our task was to obtain as much information as possible but not necessarily to engage the enemy, as one armoured carrier would not be any match against the Japanese troops.

Sitting in the carrier with the sun beating down we waited as long as we thought necessary and then with great relief we turned round and drove back, once more we had got out of what could have been a tricky situation.

It was essential for the Japanese to capture intact the oil wells for the progress of their tanks and vehicles to carry out their plans to capture Burma.

Japs advancing on the oil fields

General Slim was determined to hold the oil wells until the last possible moment, for the entire motorised transport and armour of the army was now dependent on what was produced at Yenangyaung.

There was only a limited time that the Burma Army could hold back the powerful enemy who were moving remorselessly forward all the time. If the Japs took over the oil wells before they were destroyed the forward movement would escalate and would be another nail in the coffin of Slim's forces.

Yenangyaung became a ghost town, the women and children and non-essential staff were given 12 hours to prepare for evacuation by river steamer. Once again as in the port of Rangoon and many towns it was a case of shut your front door and leave behind everything you possessed and had built up over the years not knowing whether you would ever return and if you did what state your home would be in.

On the 15th of April General Slim gave the order for the demolition of the oilfields and refinery.

A series of earth shattering explosions sent millions of gallons of crude oil up in flames. From a distance we could see columns of orange-black smoke soaring hundreds of feet into the air and the ground shuddered underfoot as machines, workshops and buildings disintegrated.

A strong enemy force had penetrated Yenangyaung itself, too late to prevent the destruction of the oil wells but in an ideal position to destroy the Burma Army if they did not move fast to escape.

The Japs now surrounded Yenangyaung and trapped many of our troops including the Inniskillings, the Cameroonians, the West Yorks, the Gloucesters and the Gurkhas.

I was thankful that I was not one of the trapped troops and was able to start moving back along the road to Assam.

Somehow or other the encircled British and Indian troops had to be extricated. Tanks and Infantry made a series of gallant attempts to smash the roadblocks but no sooner were they cleared than the enemy rushed in reinforcements and re-established them.

It was imperative to get the wounded through as many had been lying unattended for more than 48 hours.

General Bruce Scot ordered the destruction of all the ambulances, lorries and guns and as many of the wounded as possible were put aboard the tanks and what remained of the column struck out on foot. Many of the wounded were too sick to move and tears ran down the cheeks of men as they looked over their shoulders at the comrades they were abandoning.

After great frustration in getting the Chinese troops to attack Yenangyaung from the north, General Slim eventually got the Chinese General to go into action to relieve the Burma Army.

The fighting was bloody and intense, roadblocks were smashed only to be erected again soon after.

Eventually our troops broke through and this was to be the last great battle in Burma.

During the latter part of the withdrawal I was with a couple of my mates when we came into contact with some Chinese troops.

They were smiling and didn't seem to have a care in the world. We were impressed with their automatic pistols, which they all seemed to carry.

As they were so friendly one of my mates asked them if he could handle one of their pistols.

Although speech was a problem we overcame this with sign language and they laughed and handed over one of their pistols.

One of my mates held the pistol with great care in case it was loaded and we were very impressed with it.

We were suddenly shocked when a bullet from the pistol was fired and hit a Chinese lad in the stomach. It could have been any of us that were shot but he dropped to the ground screaming in great pain.

We felt in danger as they could have turned nasty over the shooting but strangely they were still smiling and picked up the soldier and carried him away to the medical centre.

Once again we had extricated ourselves from what could have been a serious incident. I gripped my rifle with great relief and moved swiftly away from the area.

Things were now getting really tough. We had little ammunition, our clothes were torn and salt-encrusted with dry sweat, our boots had worn out and a lot of the men were wearing slippers.

I was surprised when I saw General Alexander crossing the river Chindwin at Kalewa. On reaching the other side he strode out smartly, immaculately dressed as always, and a General that we had great confidence in.

I covered the last few hundred miles by whatever means I could, marching or getting a lift in any vehicle around.

One day as I walked along the road with a pal of mine from the "Dukes", we came across a 3-ton truck that had been abandoned.

Curiosity got the better of us and we tried to work out why it had been dumped. I could drive so I got behind the steering wheel and to my amazement the engine started.

With a grin on our faces we settled into the truck and I put it in gear, let out the clutch and low and behold it moved forward.

This was better than walking so why not take advantage. After about a mile I decided to stop and assess our situation.

I applied the foot brake again and again but nothing happened and I quickly realised why the truck had been left on the side of the road.

As I was not going very fast the truck came to a stop and we looked at each other in disbelief. We thought it was too good to be true and once more we would have to sweat it out on the rough road.

I had some idea how engines worked but we were now approaching a very hilly section of the terrain.

Climbing the hills would be no problem but going down the other side was a different matter.

A plan was forming in my brain that I thought was a possibility but was it? If you leave the engine in gear and switch off the ignition the truck will slow down.

This was the theory I was working on but would it work in practice.

It was a large truck and if it ran out of control we should probably be killed and after what we had endured this would not be a fitting climax.

My pal had the option of risking his life or carry on walking, we were desperate for some help. He said he would come with me and put his life in my hands,

So off we went, fingers crossed, and soon came to a hill, which we climbed with no trouble.

Now for the crunch, I reached the peak of the hill and slowly started down the other side, which looked ominously steep.

As I gathered speed, making sure the engine was in gear, my theory was put into practice. The key to success was to switch off the ignition and as I had hoped the truck slowed down.

With great relief we looked at each other and stared skyward in thanks for this near miracle.

To get the truck moving again I pressed the clutch which disengaged the engine and then when I was going fast enough I released the clutch and the engine engaged and once more slowed us down.

This sequence of events continued until we reached the bottom of the hill.

I don't know whether the reader will believe this account of driving a 3-ton truck over a steep hill without brakes but I am alive to prove that it did work. So we pressed on enjoying this unexpected help and covered many miles.

Sometimes when I stopped the mass of refugees who were clogging the road tried everything to get a lift but I couldn't risk the extra weight and what if I crashed and killed them.

Eventually we reached the Assam border and the road was too poor to go any farther. With some help we pushed the truck to the side and into a ravine where it smashed to pieces.

This episode in the story was now finished and we marched on once more thankful for the help we had invented with our lorry.

Our escape to India might just be possible during the dry season but with the coming monsoon the situation would be drastically changed. Jungle tracks would disintegrate into muddy bogs, impassable to all vehicles including bullock-carts. Even mules would find it difficult in places to retain their footing. There would be malaria, black water fever, jaundice, typhus and the dreaded cholera; I think that's enough to go on with, don't you.

It is usual in Burma for the monsoon to arrive in the middle of May, but we would sooner be bombed by the Japanese Air Force than hear the rumble of thunderclouds heralding the monsoon.

When I arrived in Imphal the monsoon broke in torrents of rain soaking everyone and bringing out latent malaria in many of us.

You would have thought that after the terrible conditions we had to endure in Burma the battered Battalions that had lost at least fifty percent of their personnel would have been allocated reasonable accommodation, but this was not so, we were put in tatty bamboo shacks that let the rain in and our toilet was, even for us, disgusting, it consisted of a slit trench over which was suspended a bamboo pole that we had to grab hold of and pray we didn't fall in the trench, not exactly the treatment we would have expected after fighting over a thousand miles. It was said that many of the senior officers in India who had not experienced the Burma war were critical of our fighting ability and dedication, so be it, but we knew what we had been through.

From the day that the Japanese had begun the war, the first Burma campaign had lasted 163 days, just over five months.

What was left of my battalion assembled in Imphal in Assam and licked their wounds. My troubles were not yet over as I contracted my second dose of Malaria and I was very ill. I lay in a coma for several days while Indian medical staff looked after me and they were excellent. Nothing was too much trouble and I recovered and returned to the regiment.

Out of 600 troops that marched out of Peshawar Barracks on the North West Frontier six months ago only about 200 survived what was probably one of the bloodiest wars ever fought and will go down in the history of the 2nd Battalion Duke of Wellingtons as a great fighting retreat.

For the sacrifices we had made we were given six months pay and sent off to a Hill Station for a month's recuperation, which we thoroughly enjoyed.

Before going on leave, to pass the time, we played cards for money and it got a bit hectic at times as the stakes got higher. Some of the lads lost all their leave money and slunk off to their shacks.

Ranchi was where the battalion resettled and trained ready to return to Burma as Chindits when they were ready.

Not everyone understands what "Chindits" stand for so I thought I would pen a few lines to explain the task they were given. (This will mean jumping forward in time but I will return to the story in the next section).

Their leader and instigator was General Ord Wingate who gained the support of President Roosevelt of the USA and Winston Churchill.

His plan was to put troops behind the Japanese lines and destroy roads and railways in order to smash their lines of communication.

Some troops would be flown in when strips had been cleared to take their planes and gliders, while others marched, taking all their supplies with them, helped by mules doing a terrific job.

The operation was known as "Thursday" and was due to be launched on 5 March 1944.

Tragedy struck nineteen days after the launch when General Wingate was killed as his plane crashed into some hills. I wonder if he looked down from above and urged his men on.

The force that Wingate put together was known as "Third Indian Division (Special Force)". It comprised six Brigades and the "Dukes" were in 23 Brigade commanded by Brigadier Perowne.

The composition of this Brigade was: 2nd Battalion The Duke of Wellington's Regiment, 4th Battalion The Border Regiment and 1st Battalion The Essex Regiment.

Owing to a desperate situation in Northern Burma this Brigade was removed by General Slim from Special Force, although it had trained as a Chindit Brigade, it was now to be used to cover the left flank of 2ⁿᵈ British Division to prevent the Japanese reaching Dimapur.

After the siege of Kohima it harassed the retreating forces of General Sato's 31ˢᵗ Japanese Division.

The Chindit training comprised of a 20-week course centred on the technique of air supply in the jungle. Number One Air Commando, commanded by Colonel Cochrane, carried out the Air Force side of the operation.

The Chindits had to form "strongholds" once flown in and if possible within 36 hours.

From these "strongholds" raiding parties could dominate the surrounding countryside and disrupt Japanese supplies and communications.

The "strongholds" were located at a place sufficiently inaccessible from main roads or railways to ensure that the enemy could not bring up tanks or heavy artillery to attack us.

There had to be a flat area large enough to create an airstrip for Dakotas so that supplies would come in and wounded flown out.

The landing strips proved more hazardous than anticipated and mostly in deep jungle surrounded by trees, which gave the glider pilots no second chance.

Every man knew exactly what was expected of him and what he had to do when he landed.

Each aircraft towed two gliders and during the pilots' training I was invited to travel in one of these gliders and it was a great experience. When taking off I watched the towrope tighten and the glider quickly lift off the ground so that I was looking down on the Dakota towing the glider.

I repeated this three mornings following and was

amazed at the smooth descent with no noise except the air rushing by.

Dakotas came in and took off in different directions on a single strip all night at the rate of one landing and one take-off every three minutes.

In a couple of days 1200 men, 2000 mules and all the necessary equipment and ammunition had been flown in.

Only a week after the launch the Chindits had totally blocked both the roads and railways, thus denying supplies and reinforcements to the forward Japanese troops, not a bad effort!

I am not sure what the "Chindits" achieved in the context of the Burma battle but they were brave and many died carrying out their orders.

Over sixty years on from the battles in Burma I assume there are not too many of the troops that took part still alive, nevertheless, should there be any soldiers who had any part to play in the campaign who have read my brief and personal account and feel that parts of the book may have deviated from the truth I sincerely apologise to them. Like you I was there and have donated my story to posterity, as there may never be such a bloody war again.

A Twist of Fate

Our base on the outskirts of Ranchi, which was in the north east of India, was situated in a wood where the Battalion was spread in Companies among the trees.

It was good for training as there was a vast amount of open countryside surrounding the wood and we were about to be trained as a mechanised unit.

Track Carriers, Jeeps and other vehicles began to pour into our camp and from foot soldiers we gradually learned how to drive and maintain the vehicles.

Driving for me was quite enjoyable, all vehicles came alike and Track Carriers were fun as they bounced over fields and any uneven ground.

We lived in tents with wooden beds to relax on. Indians set up a canteen stocked up with supplies that we readily purchased to supplement our basic meals.

For instance with a pal of mine, on some afternoons, we would send one of the young Indian lads that were hanging around the camp to the canteen to purchase a large tin of peaches and a tin of evaporated milk. When he returned we opened the tins with a bayonet and shared out the peaches and milk in our mess tins, then slowly we swallowed the contents and thought that life was great. There was a temporary end to these arrangements when the lad who we sent to the canteen failed to return with the peaches and milk and of course we lost our money as well.

Someone must have thought I had potential because I was promoted to Lance Corporal, this only meant one stripe but it was reckoned to be the hardest promotion in the British Army because you were competing against the rest of your platoon and now you were on the first rung of a ladder which ensured further promotion.

The Battalion was gradually being brought up to full strength with the addition of 400 officers and men sent from the UK.

Having lost two-thirds of the original Battalion either killed or taken prisoner it was strange to see so many new faces and those that had fought in Burma were looked on as experienced troops.

We didn't realise at the time the tragedy that had unfolded when their mothers, fathers, wives and children were informed that their loved ones had died or were prisoners of war, very sad, but this was war and we had no choice but to fight for our country although we were thousands of miles away.

No stone was left unturned to find out what had happened to any particular soldier. I was questioned many times and I told them all I knew about their movements and whether they were killed or drowned.

We spent Christmas in Ranchi and that was 1942. There was no Father Christmas or presents but our entertainment was provided by a pig which was let loose in the woods and we were told to fix bayonets and get it or there was no Christmas dinner, I didn't see the pig but I had a nice pork chop.

Transport was laid on some evenings to take us into Ranchi where my highlight was a milkshake and a meal in a Chinese restaurant.

I was given command of three track carriers and set about training the crews that would operate them.

The extra responsibility that my stripe had given me was no problem and I enjoyed giving orders to the crews.

I taught the lads how to drive and maintain our carriers and felt that I was doing something useful for a change.

The officer in charge of my platoon had only recently joined us and I listened closely to his accent, which immediately struck a chord for it was a Bristol accent. Seeing as Bristol had always been my home we struck up a friendly relationship and often spoke of our hometown.

After a few months training we became quite proficient with our carriers and we were involved in a competition in which all the Companies participated.

The judges were a Brigadier and our new Commanding Officer, Colonel "Bull" Faithful, who was a tough looking man and had boxed for the Army and was a very good rugby player.

I watched carefully as the competition progressed and by the time I had to move my three carriers to the designated starting area I felt confident my crews would do well.

We approached as quietly as possible to the side of a hill, which overlooked another hill about 600 yards away.

I ordered my three Bren gunners to get out of the carriers and line up their Bren guns on the opposite hill where a puff of smoke would give the clue to the target.

With magazines on and safety catches off I gave the orders to my number one gun: Target 600 yards; Copse; 2 o'clock; one burst of machine gun fire. If the gun was off target I adjusted my fire orders and tried again. When I was on target I gave the order: "All guns rapid fire".

It was most impressive with the three Brens firing together. After emptying the magazines I switched to the next target and repeated the sequence. There were three targets and I was very impressed by the control I had over the reliable Bren guns. Now we moved quickly back to the carriers and returned to our parking area.

I believe the reason my crews were so successful was that I had gone over and over in my mind the procedure I would follow and briefed my lads accordingly.

The Battalion now assembled in a large open space and waited for the Colonel to tell us how we had performed in the competition.

Colonel Faithful was not one to hold back on criticising us when he knew lives could be lost by bad decisions.

I stood by my carrier wondering what the Colonel would have to say. I was well satisfied with my contribution to the competition and felt quite relaxed.

I don't remember his exact words but suddenly I took great interest as he said: "I was most impressed by the control and performance of one of our junior NCOs and that was Lance Corporal Nicholls who I would like to step forward". I couldn't believe what I was hearing and in a daze I marched smartly up to the Colonel and saluted. "Well done Corporal", he said, "you did a fine job and I would like to reward you with five rupees out of my own pocket".

In front of the Battalion I saluted, turned round, and marched back. This was the Colonel of a great regiment who I had never spoken to before and I felt elated and satisfied that I had thought it all out before we went into action.

If life had not taken a sudden dramatic turn I feel sure that I would very soon have been climbing the promotion ladder and even a commission was not out of the question.

Our training continued as we attacked imaginary targets and learned to handle our carriers quite proficiently.

One morning our Company put in an attack on a village

that was supposed to be occupied by the enemy. My three track carriers moved up to the edge of the village and I gave the order to dismount and line up the Bren guns ready to fire when a target appeared.

After a short time I gave the order to withdraw the Bren guns and load up the carriers.

As we drove away from the village something happened that would change my life. Call it fate or what you like but the next few minutes were to put an end to my front line action against the Japanese. If it had not happened I would most surely have gone into action in Northern Burma and possibly killed.

We were travelling at about twenty miles an hour over rough country when in a flash a wide trench appeared in front of us.

Only seconds were left to make the decision whether to try and stop or jump the trench which track carriers were capable of doing.

I had to decide and I shouted to my driver: "jump it", he put his foot hard on the accelerator and we took off. The carrier was short of the far side of the trench and hit the edge with an almighty bang. We shot up in the air and crashed down on the far side. My driver was OK as he had some support.

In a flash I crashed back down on to a piece of steel that the Bren gun normally rested on. The metal went straight through my left thigh and smashed the bone. My men dragged me out of the carrier and laid me on the ground. Blood poured out of my leg and shirts were being torn up and wrapped round to try and stem the bleeding.

We didn't carry much medical equipment so I had to be taken to hospital as soon as possible before I bled to death.

The only suitable transport for conveying me to Ranchi

hospital was an open truck. Having stemmed the bleeding with makeshift bandages and tied my legs together as in the First Aid manual I was carefully lifted on to the back of a truck.

To get back to the main road the driver had to negotiate several paddy fields that were surrounded by mounds of earth and the truck had to go over these obstacles and drop down on the other side with a bump.

When you have a fractured femur the slightest movement causes excruciating pain so that bumping over a mound of earth was almost unbearable and I yelled out several times.

After what seemed an age we arrived at Ranchi hospital where a surgeon and his team took me into the theatre and started to operate.

Owing to the tropical climate putting my leg in plaster was not an option. While I was under the anaesthetic my shinbone was drilled and a thick metal pin inserted. I was then put in a wooden bed on my back where a goal post contraption was placed from the bottom to the top. A pulley was fixed on the bottom post and a cord was tied to the pin in my shin, passed over the pulley and then tied on to a small sack of sand.

The weight of sand had to be sufficient to pull the cord attached to my shin so that the fractured bones were just kept apart. My leg was raised in a splint, which was probably to keep the circulation moving.

When the bones are kept apart they will gradually knit together and every week an x-ray was taken and depending on the position of the broken bones a small amount of sand was taken out of the sack to allow the healing process to continue.

This may sound a crude form of surgery and many of the troops were amazed when they came to visit me. Believe it or not I was in this goalpost contraption for nine months before the femur bone, which is the thickest in the body, was strong enough to take my weight.

After nine months on my back with my leg at an upward angle you can imagine the wonderful relief when the goalpost contraption was dismantled and I was able to lie on my side, something we take for granted had suddenly become a wonderful experience for me.

Having said my goodbyes to the hospital staff I travelled several hundred miles to a convalescing hospital where a medical board decided that I was not fit for the Infantry and changed my Army grade from A1 to C3.

Joining the Royal Signals

After a month getting fit at a Hill Station in the north of India which was overlooked by the Himalayas I was told to report to Bangalore which had a lovely climate at 2000 feet above sea level.

About twenty lads from different Battalions and Units arrived at this camp wondering what the Army was about to train them for.

When we had settled in we assembled in a type of classroom where the instructor gave us tests on all sorts of subjects, mostly written questions.

After a few days we were told how we had faired in the tests and I had done well enough to be chosen for a cipher course.

For several months those selected were taught the intricacies of the cipher machines and how to use more simple codes when in the forward areas. Cipher was only used in safe base areas as the loss of one of these machines to the enemy would be catastrophic and would mean a court martial for those involved. When the course finished and I was a qualified Cipher Operator I was sent to a Signals unit in Doolalhi near Bombay.

It was good here and after the tough infantry training that I had experienced since being called up it was a total change with 12-hour office shifts night and day working on the latest cipher machines.

The Indian Captain in charge of the Cipher Unit must have been satisfied with my work as he had me promoted to Corporal that meant two stripes and an increase in pay.

We were on standby to move up to Northern Burma where the Japanese were pouring in trying to break through the 14th Army front line and drive on to India.

Before we moved up to where the action was about to explode a week's break in Bombay was on offer so we boarded a train after a few gin and limes at the station, this was the only drink available at this time and very nice it was too.

It was very hot in Bombay but it didn't stop us doing a bit of sightseeing, the Gateway to India was a magnificent sight and a visit to an air-conditioned cinema was enjoyable but coming out was like walking into a greenhouse.

Early one morning the unit positioned itself on the road with sufficient transport to take us all the way to Calcutta, this was a thousand miles right across India and as I could drive I was given charge of one of the many vehicles.

We drove for two days and then camped for a day for vehicle maintenance and to clean ourselves up and wash some of our clothes. This sequence went on until we reached Calcutta where our old trucks were changed for brand new American trucks in which we drove on to Chittagong in Northern Burma.

Having set up our equipment we started taking messages from the front line troops and passed on this information to the Airforce. They loaded up their planes with supplies that were required and then dropped them by parachute.

After four years in the Far East the Army decided that I had had enough and I set off for a transit camp outside Bombay where my papers were processed and after a medical I was able to board a ship where I saw what some troops described as the finest sight in their lives and that was the Gateway to India from the stern of a ship!

It was very relaxing as we crossed the Indian Ocean and headed for Suez laying on the deck soaking up the sun.

We were not able to use the Suez Canal on the way out but now with the European war nearly over the shorter trip to the Mediterranean Sea was available and we took it.

From the Red Sea the amazing piece of engineering takes you through Egypt to Port Said an experience not to be missed.

As we sailed through the Mediterranean an announcement from the Captain stated that the Germans were defeated and the European war was over. A bottle of beer was issued to all the troops on board and we toasted the victory.

Passing Gibraltar we sailed through the Bay of Biscay and headed for Liverpool thankful to arrive back in one piece.

We watched the boats sailing up the Mersey before we disembarked on my birthday, May 25th 1945 and I was 25.

Thinking back it seemed a coincidence that I swam the River Sittang on my daughter's birthday the 23rd February and I arrived back on my birthday.

By train I travelled to Rippon in Yorkshire where I was given a travel warrant and issued with a new set of kit.

Home after five years travelling thousands of miles I was happy to see my family and they were pleased to see me.

My father told me he had received a telegram in 1942 stating that I was missing, which at the time was quite true. He didn't tell anyone else and was very relieved when the Army confirmed that I was safe.

After an enjoyable four weeks leave, much of it spent in the local public house, I returned to Rippon where the Army considered what to do with me now that the European war was over.

The war in Burma that I had now left behind, was in full swing and the "Dukes" were fighting for their lives as the Japanese refused to give up the fight to break through to India.

The Battalion was now in Northern Burma, fighting on the flank of 2nd British Division where I understand they did a very good job although they suffered severe casualties. Whether any of my pals lost their lives in these battles I don't know, but I hope they survived and eventually were reunited with their families. Due to circumstances beyond my control I was not involved in these battles and once again I survived.

After a short respite I was given a travel warrant to Germany, which was in ruins after the continual bombing and as the train crawled through the outskirts of Hamburg the smoke was still coming up from the desolate buildings and people were picking up anything of value they could lay their hands on.

A few short weeks in Germany and I waited anxiously to see where I would be posted to continue my cipher career.

Surprise, surprise, I couldn't believe my eyes, it was Paris, a city I had only dreamed of visiting.

Nine months in Paris, working in a Cipher Office attached to the British Embassy was a just reward for the time I had spent in Burma.

I was able to visit all the wonderful things that Paris is famous for, the list goes on and on, Eiffel Tower, Pigalle, Champs Elysee, River Seine, it was a great experience.

I was asked to take a train to Toulon to join the cipher office there and after an all night journey I arrived at the resort on the Riviera.

Caught on camera in a street in Paris in 1946

There was a slight hiccup when the train stopped at Marseilles. I noticed on the far side of the station that American volunteers were giving away free doughnuts to the troops. I dashed over as fast as I could and eagerly picked up my goodies. When I turned round I was shocked to see my train pulling out of the station with all my kit on board. Next day I continued my journey and was very relieved to find my kit on Toulon station.

I must have been "potty" to attempt this!

As there was not a lot of cipher work there I was given a Jeep and told to travel to Marseilles, along the coast road, and pick up the mail, this was a daily routine, which I thoroughly enjoyed.

The scenery on the French coast was stunning and as I passed the partially submerged French warships, that we had sunk early in the war to stop them falling into German hands, I could not imagine the devastation that our battleships had inflicted on the French.

Sergeants' Mess in Paris

Just about to set off to pick up the mail in a Jeep

Back to Paris to continue my cipher work and to accept my third stripe which made me a sergeant.

Several times I went on leave to Bristol travelling on the ferry across the Channel.

The hectic life style I was leading in Paris came to an end and I was discharged from the Army after six years, most of which I must confess I found very stimulating and would not have missed for anything.

I married Barbara in 1947 and we have now been married 57 years. We had three children, Steven, Val and Jackie.

There are six Grandchildren, Daniel, Tom, Michele, Matthew, Debbie and Lisa who have all made great lives for themselves.

At the present time there are four Great Grandchildren, Ella, Molly, Ben, Charlie and one more due very shortly.

Appendix Memorials to fallen comrades

In Memory of
Lieutenant Colonel HERBERT BASIL OWEN

562, Cdg. 2nd Bn., Duke of Wellington's (West Riding Regt.)
who died age 39
on 23 February 1942
Son of Herbert and Mary Owen; husband of Betty
Owen.

Remembered with honour
TAUKKYAN WAR CEMETERY

Commemorated in perpetuity by
the Commonwealth War Graves Commission

In Memory of
Captain JOHN ANTHONY ALEXANDER
CHRISTISON

85908, 2nd Bn., Duke of Wellington's
(West Riding Regt.)
who died age 23
on 07 March 1942
Captain CHRISTISON, Son of General
Sir Alexander Frank Philip Christison,
4th Bt., G.B.E., C.B., D.S.O., M.C.,
and of Lady Christison (nee Mitchell), of Melrose,
Roxburghshire.

Remembered with honour
RANGOON WAR CEMETERY

Commemorated in perpetuity by
the Commonwealth War Graves Commission

In Memory of
Captain JOHN LAWRENCE SMYTH

182131, 1st Bn., The Queen's Royal Regt
(West Surrey)
who died age 22
on 07 May 1944
Captain SMYTH, Son of Brigadier John George
Smyth,
V.C., M.C., M.P., and of Margaret Smyth
(nee Dundas), of Westminster, London.

Remembered with honour
RANGOON MEMORIAL

Commemorated in perpetuity by
the Commonwealth War Graves Commission

In Memory of
Private BARNETT ABRAMSON

**4626478, 2nd Bn., Duke of Wellington's
(West Riding Regt.)**

**who died age 28
on 03 April 1943
Private ABRAMSON, Son of Isaac Joseph and
Lily Abramson, of Leeds, Yorkshire.**

**Remembered with honour
RANGOON WAR CEMETERY**

**Commemorated in perpetuity by
the Commonwealth War Graves Commission**

In Memory of
Private EDWARD ALBERT BAILEY

**4626331, 2nd Bn., Duke of Wellington's
(West Riding Regt.)**

**who died age 27
on 23 February 1942**

**Remembered with honour
RANGOON MEMORIAL**

**Commemorated in perpetuity by
the Commonwealth War Graves Commission**

In Memory of
Private HARRY THORPE OLDFIELD

4626484, 2nd Bn., Duke of Wellington's
(West Riding Regt.)

who died age 31
between 22 February 1942 and 23 February 1942
Private OLDFIELD, Son of Christopher James
Oldfield and Laura Oldfield; husband of Mary Ellen
Oldfield, of Acomb, York. School Teacher.

Remembered with honour
RANGOON MEMORIAL

Commemorated in perpetuity by
the Commonwealth War Graves Commission